"First, I welcome a book on Non-Constituency Members of Parliament. The scheme is 40 years old and a book on it is overdue. This book complements Anthea Ong's excellent book on Nominated Members of Parliament. Taken together, the two books make an important contribution to our understanding of the Singapore Parliament and political governance in Singapore."

Professor Tommy Koh
Special Adviser, Institute of Policy Studies
National University of Singapore

"My friends Jenn Jong and Hoe Yeong have put together an important book about a key aspect of our Parliament and Constitution. There is an expectation that, as the Singapore electorate evolves, so must our electoral system and Constitution. To ensure that the best decisions are made when it comes to that evolution, it is critical to understand the history, fundamental motivations and effects that the NCMP scheme has and continues to have. This book is an important reading for all Singaporeans and those who wish to better understand politics in Singapore."

Nicholas Fang
Former Nominated Member of Parliament

"The NCMP scheme remains an issue that is raised and debated at every general election since it was introduced in 1984. Before reading this book, I harboured the view that the scheme inherently works against the long-term good of the opposition in Singapore. Now, I side with one of the architects of the scheme and a contributor to the book, Emeritus Senior Minister Goh Chok Tong, that it is a kind of insurance scheme for democracy. I also agree with Walter Woon, instead of considering NCMPs to be 'also-rans', they should be recognised as representing the voters who did not vote for the ruling party. These views run contrary to the conclusion of the book, written by Loke Hoe Yeong and Yee Jenn Jong. But the spirit of the book allows for many views, which is why I enjoyed reading and also learning about the Singapore Parliament and political governance in Singapore from the different narratives."

Woon Tai Ho
Channel NewsAsia founding editor and author

"This book is a great resource that captures the debate surrounding this scheme from many different voices. The NCMP scheme in its current form does not come close to addressing the huge and potentially de-stabilising gap between Opposition seats in Parliament and the Opposition's share of the popular vote. Were it not for this, it is unlikely that the People's Action Party (PAP), which has said that growing the Opposition is not its priority, would have retained the scheme. To seriously address that gap, the playing field needs to be made less unlevel. But to move beyond being a small presence in Parliament, the Opposition needs to go beyond being good NCMPs and MPs, important as that is. It needs to convince voters to embrace a viable end-goal — to first remove the PAP's parliamentary supermajority and then one day present itself as an alternative government. That would be the ultimate stabiliser for Singapore politics."

Leon Perera
Former Non-Constituency Member of Parliament and
Former Member of Parliament for Aljunied GRC

"This is a most timely volume — conspectus, commentary and critique — all in one. A must read for anyone vaguely interested in Singapore politics."

Kevin Y.L. Tan
Adjunct Professor, Faculty of Law,
National University of Singapore

"Any serious student of Singapore politics will find this book a useful and timely addition to the field. The Non-Constituency Member of Parliament (NCMP) scheme is a mainstay in our current political system and is thus worthy of such an analysis. A unique thing about this book is that it is edited by a former NCMP and an academic; having both a practitioner's and an analyst's perspectives makes it much richer and sharper, in my opinion, as both of them complement each other. The book also features thoughtful pieces by other academics and observers. The editors have done a good job in ensuring that different perspectives are put forth in it, from those who are supportive of retaining the scheme to those who are more sceptical of it. It is this diversity of thought that ultimately makes this book a compelling read."

Walid Jumblatt Bin Abdullah
Assistant Professor, School of Social Sciences,
Nanyang Technological University

NON-CONSTITUENCY MEMBERS OF PARLIAMENT

WHAT'S NEXT FOR THE SCHEME?

NON-CONSTITUENCY MEMBERS OF PARLIAMENT

WHAT'S NEXT FOR THE SCHEME?

EDITED BY

LOKE HOE YEONG
YEE JENN JONG

W World Scientific

NEW JERSEY · LONDON · SINGAPORE · BEIJING · SHANGHAI · HONG KONG · TAIPEI · CHENNAI · TOKYO

Published by

World Scientific Publishing Co. Pte. Ltd.

5 Toh Tuck Link, Singapore 596224

USA office: 27 Warren Street, Suite 401-402, Hackensack, NJ 07601

UK office: 57 Shelton Street, Covent Garden, London WC2H 9HE

National Library Board, Singapore Cataloguing in Publication Data
Name(s): Loke, Hoe Yeong, editor. | Yee, Jenn Jong, editor.
Title: Non-Constituency Members of Parliament : what's next for the scheme? /
    edited by Loke Hoe Yeong, Yee Jenn Jong.
Description: Singapore : World Scientific Publishing Co. Pte. Ltd., [2024]
Identifier(s): ISBN 978-981-12-9293-4 (hardcover) | ISBN 978-981-12-9380-1 (paperback) |
    ISBN 978-981-12-9294-1 (ebook for institutions) |
    ISBN 978-981-12-9295-8 (ebook for individuals)
Subject(s): LCSH: Singapore--Politics and government. | Democracy--Singapore. |
    Singapore. Parliament--Officials and employees. | Legislators--Singapore.
Classification: DDC 320.95957--dc23

British Library Cataloguing-in-Publication Data
A catalogue record for this book is available from the British Library.

The drawings of personalities on the front cover and appendix are copyright of
The Learning Grid Pte Ltd and illustrated by Dillon Chua.

For any available supplementary material, please visit
https://www.worldscientific.com/worldscibooks/10.1142/13831#t=suppl

Desk Editor: Jiang Yulin

Typeset by Stallion Press
Email: enquiries@stallionpress.com

Printed in Singapore

Contents

Foreword

I thank Loke Hoe Yeong and Yee Jenn Jong for inviting me to contribute the foreword for their book on Non-Constituency Members of Parliament. I wish to make four comments on the book.

First, I welcome a book on Non-Constituency Members of Parliament. The scheme is 40 years old and a book on it is overdue. This book complements Anthea Ong's excellent book on Nominated Members of Parliament. Taken together, the two books make an important contribution to our understanding of the Singapore Parliament and political governance in Singapore.

Second, I was not aware until I read this book that Singapore did not invent the scheme. In fact, we borrowed the idea from Mauritius. In Mauritius, the best losing candidate gets a seat in the Parliament.

Third, when the scheme was first introduced in 1984, it was rejected by the opposition parties. They subsequently changed their minds and supported the scheme. To date, 12 persons have served as NCMPs. Of the 12, four of them were subsequently elected to Parliament. This scheme is therefore helpful to the opposition parties.

Fourth, I like Professor Walter Woon's essay in the book. He observed that, at our past general elections, the opposition parties had won between 30% and 40% of the popular vote. However, because of our first-past-the-post system, they do not get 30–40% of the seats in

Parliament. In Professor Woon's view, the NCMPs can be said to represent the voters who did not vote for the governing party. This gives legitimacy to the standing of NCMPs.

I wish the book success.

Professor Tommy Koh,
Special Adviser, Institute of Policy Studies
National University of Singapore

Preface

To its proponents, the Non-Constituency Member of Parliament (NCMP) scheme has been an extraordinary instance of the People's Action Party (PAP) government's magnanimity in allowing 'best losers' from among candidates of opposition parties to enter Parliament. To cynics, the scheme was designed to stave off the challenge to the PAP's candidates at elections, by guaranteeing voters a minimum level of opposition representation in Parliament.

Regardless of one's perspective, the innovation of the NCMP scheme over the past four decades has been central in the management of political representation in Singapore. It may not have been an original invention, insofar as there existed the example of Mauritius in recognising the place of 'best losers' in Parliament — a precedent to which reference was made a number of times when the PAP introduced the NCMP scheme. Nevertheless, the NCMP scheme has since turned out to be among the dominant issues featuring in general elections in a way, arguably, unlike any other country.

For the PAP, the NCMP scheme has been about designing and evolving a scheme to accommodate political plurality in Parliament. More and more Singaporeans may vote for the opposition to ensure checks-and-balances in Parliament, even if a majority of them still want the PAP in government; nevertheless, the "freak election result" of the PAP losing power is entirely possible. The NCMP scheme was designed as such to act as a "stabiliser" for Singapore's first-past-the-post electoral system, in the words of former prime minister Goh Chok Tong. The PAP's leaders, not least the first prime minister Lee Kuan Yew himself, have on occasions also articulated a vision of Singapore's future that transcends party politics. Most recently in 2018, Prime Minister Lee Hsien Loong said that the PAP "does not have a monopoly of power" and "does not have the right to rule Singapore indefinitely;" and if the PAP were ever unable to renew itself and bring progress, "we deserve to lose."[1]

For the opposition, they have consistently highlighted the unlevel playing field in national politics that they face. Their supporters, as well as Singaporeans who believe in the importance of political plurality and in a counterbalance against the PAP's parliamentary supermajority, have generally concurred. In this, the opposition's grievances have ranged from what they believe to be the unfair coverage of them in the state-dominated media, to being the target of libel suits from PAP leaders.

Yet when presented with the NCMP scheme in 1984, the opposition were initially compelled to dismiss it. Having campaigned on the primacy of democratic values, they had to grapple with questions of democratic legitimacy that arose from the NCMP scheme. For how could 'losers' in an election still enter Parliament? Yet along the way, realpolitik demanded that they took advantage of the NCMP scheme in their quest to make greater inroads into Parliament. Insofar as the NCMP scheme was afforded to them as a crutch, there was also perhaps the issue of pride. NCMPs would have to address the indictment that they had entered Parliament — in the words of J. B. Jeyaretnam, the former leader of the Workers' Party — "by the grace of the government".

Fundamentally, this book is also very much about the arguments around the form and substance of Singapore's democracy that the PAP government has sought to build, and which the opposition have sought to challenge or refine, over the past four decades. This calls for a debate that ought to rise above the rough and tumble of party politics.

This debate lends itself very well as the topic for this present book, which seeks to break new ground in the annals of Singapore politics. We believe it is the first time in Singapore that members of the PAP and the opposition parties have contributed their voices to one book, alongside political observers, academics, and the media.

Why is this so important? We find ourselves in an age where political polarisation in some countries has torn them apart. This renders any dialogue across the political aisle impossible, precluding any possibility of a common public sphere. We hope Singapore never finds itself in such a position, and that the PAP and the opposition will always be guided by the mantra of "agreeing to disagree".

This book seeks to lay out the genesis of the NCMP scheme, and trace its development and evolution of Singapore's political system to the present day. In doing so, we cover some of the following key debates and questions:

— Constitutionally, how can we understand the NCMP scheme in relation to debates on how 'alternative voices' could be introduced into Parliament?
— Politically, to what extent can we understand the NCMP scheme as the result of the increasing electoral challenge to the PAP since the 1980s?

This is also a book to record and remember the contributions of a group of Singaporeans in the political life of the nation — the NCMPs Singapore has had — and to reflect on their role, whatever one's political inclination.

The book is a non-partisan one, whose purpose is to engender a balanced conversation on the NCMP scheme. It is not endorsed by any political party.

There will no doubt be difficult parts of political history where the PAP and opposition will never see eye to eye, whatever the case — we think, for instance, of the bitter altercations between J. B. Jeyaretnam and the PAP leaders. We have also been careful not to assume that the opposition is a monolithic whole, and we have tried to capture the spectrum of views where the context calls for that. We see it as our mission to present these issues in as balanced a manner as is possible, for readers to make up their own minds.

I am delighted to have been co-editor of this book with Jenn Jong. Having known him for over 10 years, including the time during which he himself served as an NCMP, I have known Jenn Jong to be an unassuming, amenable person, whose exterior belies a passion for contributing to national life and its debates. I am grateful to the contributors to this book — to Emeritus Senior Minister Goh Chok Tong for graciously agreeing to have his article on NCMPs published in this book; to Professor Tommy Koh for his foreword; to former Attorney-General Walter Woon for contributing the chapter on the constitutional issues; and to the NCMPs and former PAP MP Inderjit Singh who agreed to be interviewed — without whom this whole undertaking may not see the light of day. Acknowledgements must also go to our publisher World Scientific for supporting such an endeavour — for engendering this and other important debates on Singapore politics.

Loke Hoe Yeong
March 2024

When Chua Hong Koon of World Scientific told me that they were publishing a book on Nominated Members of Parliament (NMPs) and asked me to lead an effort to write a book about Non-Constituency Members of Parliament (NCMPs), my first reaction was, "NMPs and NCMPs are worlds apart in the arena of Singapore politics. Will a book on NCMPs have a story to tell?"

NCMPs are by design, losing candidates in Singapore's general elections, albeit best-scorers who had missed out on being elected and if the minimum number of opposition MPs was not achieved at the elections. There were few NCMPs offered the post since the scheme was first started in the General Election of 1984. In contrast, Parliament currently provides for around nine NMPs each time, and there are typically two NMP terms per election cycle. NMPs are by design, non-political, although some have been members of the ruling party before but will need to resign before applying to be NMPs. Most of them were nominated by a particular functional group though they represent themselves when they are in Parliament, unlike NCMPs who remain active and are often senior members of an opposition party. There are therefore many times more NMPs than NCMPs. It would be much easier to get NMPs to write about their term in Parliament and areas that they are passionate about.

NCMPs are very different. While the parliamentary duties of NCMPs and NMPs are designed to be the same, NCMPs are part of a democratic political process that is adversarial in nature. They need to contest gruelling general elections against a very dominant ruling party who designed the electoral system, including that of the NCMP scheme. They have a longer longevity as politicians look to contest in several general elections, each four to five years apart, and perhaps occasionally in by-elections. As one of the better performers amongst a large field of opposition candidates in the general elections, they tend to have higher public profiles, and some even have highly publicised clashes with the ruling party.

Nevertheless, I thought it was an interesting suggestion. No book has ever been written specifically about the NCMP scheme or about the NCMPs as an entire group before. The scheme itself evolved out of Singapore's unique political system, where the ruling party once had absolute control over Parliament from 1968 but had started to see a small handful of opposition candidates making breakthroughs in the 1980s. The NCMP scheme is one of several uniquely Singapore inventions, alongside that of the Group Representation Constituency (GRC), Town Councils, Elected Presidency, NMPs amongst others. It was once relevant, at least to the ruling party who had mooted this scheme. That was when there were few opposition candidates who were able to directly defeat their PAP opponents in the elections, and yet there was a strong demand by Singaporeans for alternative voices in Parliament. The opposition parties oppose the NCMP scheme, yet in the dynamics of Singapore politics, the majority who were offered this post ended up accepting the very scheme which they opposed. I was once part of this dilemma too and became an NCMP. I come from a political party that has the largest number being offered the position.

Why write the book now? My personal conviction from two decades of following politics from afar and over a decade of being in the thick of the action, is that Singapore politics is changing. We are presently going into the fourth-generation leadership of the PAP. The opposition candidates are quite different from that of the 1980s when the scheme and many other political innovations were created. The electorates have become very different too. In General Election 2020, the opposition won 10 seats. Sengkang GRC was won by the Workers' Party without any experienced parliamentarian in the team. Opposition parties have closed the gap on the PAP and are slowly breaking down the fortresses that have been enacted. The NCMP scheme is designed to become irrelevant if the number of opposition MPs exceeds the threshold, currently set at 12.

In that respect, it is an opportune time to look at the 40 years of the NCMP scheme, its role in our evolving political scene and at the 16 persons who had either served as NCMPs or were offered the position. Since Sylvia Lim became the first NCMP to be elected as an MP, there have now been three more who went on to be MPs. We could well be looking at a scheme that has come to the tail-end of its relevance and we might be seeing the last of the NCMPs of Singapore. To me, that is worth a story to tell.

It is also my privilege to write the book with Hoe Yeong whom I had first met 10 years ago as a result of my political work. Hoe Yeong has himself written bestselling books about the opposition in Singapore. He was very meticulous and sharp in commenting on the draft version of my own book, *Journey in Blue: A Peek into the Workers' Party of Singapore*. Even the title of my book was modified for the better due to his suggestion!

I also wish to thank former NMP and former Attorney-General Walter Woon and former political desk journalist Ng Wai Mun for contributing a chapter each to the book. I have always held Walter in high regard for his active contributions as an NMP and for his incisive writings. Being a respected legally trained person, his contribution has offered good insights on the constitutional aspects of the scheme. Wai Mun had interviewed me several times before when she was a journalist. We were pleased when she agreed so readily to help with this book. Many thanks to everyone who had contributed their opinions so that we could have views from across the political spectrum and from interested observers. Like Hoe Yeong, I hope that this book will help to contribute to Singapore evolving a working political system without the extreme divisiveness seen elsewhere.

Yee Jenn Jong
March 2024

About the Editors

Loke Hoe Yeong is the author of *The First Wave: JBJ, Chiam & the Opposition in Singapore*, a history of the opposition since 1984. He is currently Head of Research at a trade association in the City of London.

Yee Jenn Jong is an author, politician, entrepreneur and a former Non-Constituency Member of Parliament (NCMP). He is also the author of the bestseller *Journey in Blue: A Peek into the Workers' Party of Singapore*. As an active participant in Singapore's political scene at a time when the opposition started to entrench itself into the political system as well as a former NCMP, Jenn Jong is able to offer unique perspectives on this topic.

About the Contributors

Walter Woon, SC, served as the fifth Attorney-General of Singapore between 2008 and 2010. He was a Nominated Member of Parliament from 1992 to 1996. Professor Woon has also served as the Ambassador of Singapore to Germany, Greece, the European Union, Belgium, Luxembourg, the Netherlands and the Vatican. He is currently the Lee Kong Chian Visiting Professor at the Yong Pung How School of Law, Singapore Management University, and is Emeritus Professor at the National University of Singapore.

Ng Wai Mun is a former political correspondent with the Chinese-language daily *Lianhe Zaobao*, with a decade of experience covering elections and local politics. She is now deputy editor at a regional sustainability publication.

1

The Non-Constituency Member of Parliament Scheme
The Constitutional Position

Walter Woon

The Singapore Parliament was for a long time dominated by a single party, viz, the People's Action Party (PAP). Their monopoly of legislative power was broken by the election of J. B. Jeyaretnam in the Anson by-election on 31 October 1981. This event was not greeted with much graciousness by the powers-that-were. It led to the realisation that the electorate could not be counted on to keep electing the PAP indefinitely. The result was the introduction of the scheme to allow members of the opposition to enter Parliament notwithstanding that they had failed to secure a seat in a general election.

It is vital to understand that the first-past-the-post system adopted in Singapore is not the only method for choosing Members of Parliament (MP). The reason that we have it here is because Singapore was a British colony. The British modelled Singapore's parliamentary system after their own. The Westminster system allows a candidate to be elected to Parliament even though he/she has not received an absolute majority of the votes cast. This happens when there are more than two candidates. Three or more candidates will split the vote, and the winner will very often only receive a plurality of the votes cast.

The situation that obtained in Singapore prior to the election of Jeyaratnam in 1981 was unusual. In many cases, PAP candidates were 'elected' without a contest. Where there was a contest, usually there were only two candidates (Table 1).[1]

It will be seen from Table 1 that in most constituencies contested during the four immediate post-Independence elections there was a straight fight between the PAP and the challengers. Of necessity, in such a situation the winner will obtain a majority of the votes. Even where the non-PAP vote was split, the ruling party still managed to get a majority. There was not a single case of an MP being elected with less than 50% of the vote. It is against this backdrop that the introduction of Non-Constituency Members of Parliament (NCMPs) must be seen. The significance of this will be explained later in this chapter.

Provision for NCMPs was made in the Constitution of the Republic of Singapore (Amendment) Act 1984. At the second reading of the

Table 1:   Singapore's General Elections, 1968–80: Seats Contested

General Election	Uncontested seats	Contested seats (2 candidates)	Contested seats (more than 2 candidates)
1968	51	7	Nil
1972	8	33	24
1976	16	51	2
1980	37	33	5

amendment bill, then Prime Minister Lee Kuan Yew explained the rationale for the scheme[2]:

> "The main objective of the proposed legislation is to ensure that there will be in Parliament a minimum number of Opposition representatives. If in the general elections less than the minimum number is returned, then Opposition party candidates who poll the highest percentage of votes will be declared returned as non-constituency Members to bring the number up to the prescribed minimum. It is proposed that this minimum be three non-constituency Members. However, the number can later be increased by Parliament to six. The effect of the legislation, therefore, is that it as has happened in the past four general elections, the PAP wins all seats, there will still be in this Chamber at least three Opposition Members."

The Prime Minister went on to expand on his thinking in introducing such a scheme (with a gratuitous *ad hominem* dig at Jeyaratnam)[3]:

> "Why should we deliberately ensure that Parliament, henceforth, should have at least a few Opposition Members? There are several reasons. First, from our experience, since December 1981 when the Member for Anson entered this Chamber, we discovered that there are considerable benefits for younger Ministers and MPs. They have not faced the fearsome foes of the 1950s and 60s. Initially, they were awkward in tackling the Opposition Member. But they soon sharpened their debating skills and they have learned to put down the inanities of the Member for Anson...
>
> ... Secondly, and much more important, Opposition MPs will educate a younger generation of voters who, not having experienced the conflicts in this House in the 1950s and 60s, harbour myths about the role of an Opposition. Although they may be disillusioned by the

3

performance of the Member for Anson, some hope that other Opposition candidates can be more credible and effective. Well, let there be others. The people will learn the limits of what a constitutional Opposition can do.

Thirdly, some non-PAP MPs will ensure that every suspicion, every rumour of misconduct, will be reported to the non-PAP MPs, at least anonymously. We all know that. These MPs, unlike PAP MPs, will give vent to any allegation of misfeasance or corruption or nepotism, whereas PAP MPs know that they should only take up the matter after enquiries show that allegations have some shadow of truth. This approach of Opposition Members will dispel suspicions of cover-ups of alleged wrongdoings."

Lee went on to give his assessment of younger Singaporean voters[4]:

"Over 60% of today's voters are aged 40 and below. They were teenagers or toddlers when the struggles were enacted in the 1950s and 60s. They have no idea how destructive opposition can be. They feel that they are missing something. They want to experience some of the excitement of political combat.

Sir, we can broadly define the older political generation as those who are aged 20 and above at the time of the race riots in 1964. That is a convenient landmark in all our lives. Those aged 20 and above were old enough to experience and to remember the riots and revolution, the intimidation and assassinations, the strikes and demonstrations, the disruption and destruction in the 1950s and the 1960s. In the February 1968 elections, this politically experienced generation were 91% of the electorate. In 1972, they were 74% of the electorate. By the 1976 elections, they were 61% of the electorate. In the 1980 elections, they became a bare half, 50%. In 1984, they have

4

become a minority, 40%. And if we project this into 1988, they will be reduced to 31½% of the electorate, despite the old living longer. And this, Mr Speaker, Sir, is the nub of the matter.

I have a graph which vividly portrays graphically this relentless decline in the numbers in the electorate who personally experienced and recall the past. From 91% in 1968, in 16 years, they are 40% this year and will be 31½% in another four years. If we can distil the essence of the experience and conclusions of the older and transmit them to the younger generation, how fortunate would we not be? If the human mind were like computers, how marvellous it would be. The quintessence of one's generation's experience could be abstracted and fed from one brain to another. Alas, the brain works differently.

A person learns most vividly and remembers longest and best when his lessons are accompanied by sharp pain or great joy. After he has scalded himself with boiling oil, he learns how to fry more carefully the rest of his life. After he has enjoyed his first encounter with the durian, he will never forget how to identify the fragrance. Some can learn by watching others scald themselves. Few or none can learn to sniff out a good durian without having eaten both good and bad ones...

This younger generation does not know what is, or should be, an Opposition's role. Some believe that a government can be made to change its policies by vociferous protests or nagging and repetitious arguments. Others believe that they, as voters, will do boner [sic] with an Opposition pressing and coercing more benefits out of a hard-fisted government. However, not without good reason, they do not want the disadvantage of an ineffective Opposition MP in their constituency, unable to get their problems put right, from prompt repairs by HDB, PUB, TAS, to taxi and hawker licences.

By this amendment we shall provide them with some experience on the usefulness and limitations of Opposition MPs. They will experience different kinds of jousting styles and, I hope, a wider range of arguments and ideas than the limited repertoire we have got so tired of listening to since December 1981."

The bill was passed by 66 votes to one, with one abstention.[5] Thus, the main reasons for introduction of NCMPs were:

- PAP Ministers and MPs needed practical experience of dealing with an opposition;
- The voters needed to be educated about what an opposition in Parliament would be capable of doing;
- Opposition MPs would give vent to any allegations of misfeasance, corruption or nepotism;
- Younger voters should feel some pain when voting for incompetent opposition members.[6]

Of the four reasons that Mr Lee propounded, the first clearly is obsolete. Opposition members have been elected regularly, the latest batch being the largest since Independence. There is now an official Leader of the Opposition. The second reason was based on his experience of the destructive and obstructive Communist-leaning opposition of the turbulent years before Independence. However, even in 1984 Lee underestimated the sophistication of younger voters. He did not appear to realise that those younger voters who had grown up in post-Independence Singapore pledged every school day to build a democratic society based on justice and equality. It should not have surprised him that some people actually came to believe in this.[7] The fourth reason is an example of the attitude that made some people mad enough to vote for the opposing candidates, just to spite the PAP. One trusts that such attitudes have been banished for good from the minds of the ruling party.

This leaves just the third reason, to "give vent to any allegation of misfeasance or corruption or nepotism." This justification remains as true today as it was in 1984. Singaporeans are sophisticated enough to know that unchecked power tends to lead to abuse. For this reason alone, the presence of MPs from opposition parties is essential for good governance.

The lone dissenting voice speaking against the introduction of NCMPs in 1984 was Workers' Party (WP) MP Jeyaretnam. His view of the proposal was as follows[8]:

> "I say, Mr Speaker, Sir, that this Bill is a fraud on the electorate. If the Prime Minister is genuine in his desire to see Opposition Members in Parliament and therefore bring about parliamentary democracy in Singapore, then may I tell him that there are other ways of doing this, far better ways than this sham Bill... not toothless Opposition Members, as you would have them, but genuine Opposition Members chosen by the electorate, who will come here to serve the citizens of Singapore."

In the four decades since the introduction of NCMPs they have become a fixture in Parliament, albeit one that will self-destruct if ever there are sufficient directly elected opposition MPs. The current version of the Constitution provides for 12 non-constituency members to "ensure the representation in Parliament of a minimum number of Members from a political party or parties not forming the Government."[9] This has been the position since 2016, when the Constitution was amended to increase the number of NCMPs and remove the restrictions on their voting rights.[10] Thus, Jeyaretnam's categorisation of NCMPs as "toothless" is no longer the case, if it ever was. An effective slate of NCMPs can have influence far beyond their meagre numbers, especially in these days of social media.

The main criticism of NCMPs is that they are not representatives of the people because they did not win their seats under the first-past-the-post system. Underlying this is a fallacy: that those who win under that system represent the majority of the electorate. This is not so.

Consider the United Kingdom, whose Parliament is the model for those of the former British colonies including Singapore. Since 1918, there have been 28 general elections. On 18 occasions the Conservatives won the most seats; Labour had the most seats on the remaining 10 occasions.[11] Interestingly, neither Labour nor the Conservatives obtained a majority of the votes, except on one occasion in 1931 (the Conservatives managed to get 55.5%).[12] The first-past-the-post system does not mean that the party with the most seats commands the support of the majority of the electorate. Indeed, in three general elections the party with the most votes did not get the most MPs.[13]

To make things starkly clear: After the 2019 UK General Election Boris Johnson's Conservatives won a landslide victory with 365 seats, a parliamentary majority of 81.[14] However, in terms of actual votes, the Conservatives only polled 43.6%.[15] It gets worse; since voting in the UK is not compulsory (unlike in Singapore), only 67.3% of the eligible voters bothered to cast their ballots.[16] This means that the Conservative landslide was based on 29.3% of the total electorate. In other words, it is a myth that under the Westminster-style election system the party with the most seats is supported by the majority of voters.

What relevance has this to Singapore? As pointed out above, the PAP managed to win elections with an absolute majority of votes in every election until 1984 (and since). Lee does not seem to have contemplated a UK-type situation, where the ruling party gets less than 50% yet has the overwhelming majority of parliamentary seats. Were this to happen, the rulers would not have the support of the majority of the ruled. This is a recipe for instability, especially in young nations with a non-homogenous electorate.

It would be foolishly naïve to assume that we will never have a situation where the constituency MPs obtain less than 50% of the vote.[17] The 2011 Presidential Election provides a cautionary tale. There were four candidates. The winner, Dr Tony Tan, obtained 35.2% of the vote.[18] If this were to happen in a general election, the constituency would be represented by a member against whom nearly two-thirds of the electorate voted. Effectively, the majority of the electorate would be voiceless. The NCMP scheme ensures that this will not happen in Singapore. Even if the ruling party makes a clean sweep, there will always be at least 12 opposition members to give a voice to the voters who would otherwise remain mute in policymaking.

The second fallacy is that the only legitimate way to choose parliamentarians is to elect them directly. This was the nub of Jeyaretnam's criticism of the NCMP scheme at its inception and has been repeated ever since by several detractors. However, such a view is narrow and ignores the fact that many countries choose their parliamentarians by proportional representation rather than by direct election.

The Federal Republic of Germany provides an instructive example. Germany is divided into 299 constituencies distributed among the 16

Länder (federal states).[19] However, the Bundestag (Federal Parliament) consists of not only MPs directly elected in their constituencies but also those chosen from party lists in the *Länder* according to the proportion of votes obtained (the minimum requirement is that a party should obtain at least 5%, in order to keep out the small fringe parties).[20] It is entirely possible for a party to win no constituency seats and yet be represented in the Bundestag. Consider, for example, Bavaria.

The people of the *Freistaat Bayern*, the Bavarian Free State, have been Bavarians longer than they have been citizens of a united Germany, so the *Land* has a strong regional (one might even say national) consciousness. Bavaria, like Singapore, has been ruled by one dominant party for decades, the Christlich-Soziale Union (CSU). The CSU is only active in Bavaria, but is linked to the Christian Democrats (Christlich Demokratische Union Deutschlands) at the federal level.

In the 2021 Bundestag election, the CSU swept all but one of the 46 constituencies in Bavaria; the lone exception being one seat won by the Greens (Bündnis 90/Die Grünen).[21] Interestingly, none of the elected candidates obtained a majority of the votes. Indeed, the lowest winner only polled 25.7%. The 'losing' parties nonetheless had MPs chosen from the party lists — including 23 for the Social Democrats who had won no constituency seats as compared to 18 for the Greens, who had taken one seat. Other parties which had MPs despite winning no constituencies were the Freie Demokratische Partei (14), the Alternative für Deutschland (12) and Die Linke (4).

Let it be clear that I am not advocating such a system for Singapore. My point is that no one in Germany doubts the legitimacy of the MPs from the 'losing' parties. The same should be the case for the NCMPs. Instead of considering them to be 'also-rans', NCMPs should be recognised as representing the voters who did not vote for the ruling party.

Some people criticise Singapore as being undemocratic because they arrogate to themselves the right to define what democracy means. They should be ignored. In the final analysis, it is not 'democracy' as practised elsewhere in the world that counts; it is good governance. Good governance requires checks on the ruling party. The Singapore electoral system has evolved to suit Singapore's needs, values and culture. NCMPs are an important part of that system.

2

The NCMP Scheme and Its Raison d'être
A Political History

Loke Hoe Yeong

Introduction: The constitutional innovations of the 1980s

L ee Kuan Yew's introduction of the Non-Constituency Member of Parliament (NCMP) scheme in 1984 came within the context of a decade of sweeping constitutional and other changes, amid the transition of power from the People's Action Party (PAP) Old Guard to the party's second-generation leaders.

The Elected Presidency scheme was first mooted by Lee and his government in 1984, for the stated purpose of instituting a popularly elected president to safeguard Singapore's reserves and assets, as well as to protect the integrity of the public services. The Group Representation Constituency (GRC) system was introduced in 1988 as a mechanism to ensure minority representation in Parliament, while eschewing communalist politics. The Town Council Act was introduced also in 1988, to devolve more municipal responsibilities to MPs. Finally, the

Nominated Member of Parliament (NMP) scheme was introduced in 1991 to allow public-minded, talented individuals to serve in Parliament without being subject to party politics for which they may not wish to be involved, for a variety of reasons.

While Lee and his government framed these reforms as necessary for good governance and, in the case of the GRC system, to ensure minority ethnic representation in Parliament, the opposition and their supporters regarded all of them as the PAP's measures to stall the advances made by the opposition during the 1980s. They regarded the Elected Presidency scheme, initially, as a means for Lee to retain power without being subject to the vagaries of the parliamentary system. They viewed the GRC system as imposing a prohibitively high bar for opposition parties to assemble teams of able candidates — at a time when it was a challenge for opposition parties to attract sufficient numbers of credible and able candidates because of the fear of personal repercussions — to contest elections. The Town Council Act was read as an attempt to saddle opposition MPs with municipal responsibilities without the resources enjoyed by their PAP counterparts.

It is fair to say that the PAP government's stated aims for these constitutional and other changes of the 1980s, and the concerns of the opposition, both have their merits. It is in this light that this chapter provides a political history of the NCMP scheme, set against the context of the growth of the opposition in the early 1980s, after years of complete dominance of Parliament by the PAP. In doing so, this chapter sets the background for the rest of the book in assessing how the NCMP scheme has turned out, as seen against those initial expectations and intentions. It will also examine how the opposition has grappled with a scheme they had criticised in the initial years as an affront to the principle of democratic legitimacy, before they began accepting offers of NCMP seats from 1988 onwards.

Background: Jeyaretnam and the 1981 Anson by-election

Before Prime Minister Lee Kuan Yew moved the bill in July 1984 to introduce the NCMP scheme through amendments to the Constitution and to the Parliamentary Elections Act, the PAP government had been discussing it for two years. As Lee explained, the creation of the scheme was a response to J. B. Jeyaretnam of the Workers' Party (WP) winning the constituency of Anson in a by-election in 1981, which broke the PAP's monopoly of Parliament since 1966.

The Anson by-election of 1981 was called because its MP, Devan Nair, had vacated the seat to become the President of Singapore. The PAP was reasonably confident of retaining the seat — not only because no opposition politician had won a seat in any election since 1963, but also because of the PAP's strong showing of 84% in Anson at the most recent general election a year earlier.

To their shock, the PAP lost Anson to Jeyaretnam. His win had been attributed — in the PAP's own post-election analysis as well as in media commentary — to a range of reasons. There was disgruntlement among dock workers in the Blair Plain district of the constituency who were rehoused. The PAP candidate in that by-election was also deemed young, inexperienced and, because of his socio-economic status, out of touch with the average Anson voter. Furthermore, there had been a general trend among younger voters favouring greater political competition.

Lee chided the younger PAP ministers and backbenchers, to whom he left much of the Anson campaign to — not so much for complacency, but for not having been "battle-hardened" by the political conflict struggles that he and the PAP Old Guard had gone through in the 1950s and 60s.

Jeyaretnam's entry into Parliament was a novelty for many, though his time in Parliament in the early 1980s was marked by the acrimonious and personal exchanges he had with Lee.

The introduction of the scheme in July 1984

Nevertheless, Lee said he had come to conclude that Jeyaretnam's presence in Parliament was actually an "educational experience" for the younger PAP members who lacked experience with the "turbulent 1950s and 60s".

As laid out earlier in Walter Woon's chapter in this book, when Lee moved the constitutional amendments in Parliament to introduce the NCMP scheme in July 1984, he said that having an opposition in Parliament was not only educational for his backbenchers, but also for voters. They would then have "some experience on the usefulness and limitations of Opposition MPs", and a chance to judge the opposition beyond election campaigns.

He acknowledged the public perception that PAP backbenchers could not be expected to vociferously question the PAP government. Also, the cautious approach of PAP MPs meant that they would not bring allegations of corruption or nepotism into Parliament for debate; but for Lee, such allegations and suspicions needed to be dispelled, and opposition MPs had to be the ones bringing them up for debate.

While the bill that Lee tabled provided for between three to a maximum of six NMCPs, subsequent Parliaments had set the number of offers of NCMP positions made after each general election at three — and this would be declared by presidential order after each election — until the legislative changes of 2010.[1] Lee contended that it was a "risk" that the opposition would then "grow in stature and influence" at the expense of the PAP — noting that the PAP itself had grown from just three Assemblymen from its maiden electoral outing in 1955. Nevertheless, NCMPs would not be given the right to vote on constitutional amendments, supply bills or motion of no confidence in the government, because, as Lee put it, "is logical and right that only elected constituency Members should vote on these critical matters."[2]

The PAP had considered other options to meet its stated goal of letting in controlled numbers of opposition members in Parliament, without being a detriment to itself. It was felt that introducing a proportional representation system of politics would only result in unstable coalition governments as in Italy. On the other hand, introducing a second chamber of Parliament was too substantial a change to Singapore's political system, which they felt was working well. The option of a 'best losers' scheme of NCMPs was judged as the simplest proposal which voters could understand.

Jeyaretnam's response in Parliament was to immediately oppose the scheme. He questioned the "haste" in which the government introduced the scheme — noting that a general election was widely expected to be called later that same year — as well as the PAP's motives, calling the scheme "a trick... a ploy on the plan of the Government." While he did not say so, implicit in Jeyaretnam's argument was that the PAP was introducing the NCMP scheme to allay the desire of voters to have some opposition presence in Parliament, but not to the extent that it would threaten the PAP's dominance, or perhaps even its ability to form the government.

Therefore, Jeyaretnam argued for a whole list of demands, if the PAP were sincere about having opposition in Parliament as it claimed — more TV and media airtime, permission to stage public rallies (outside of election time), removing the threat of detention without trial under the Internal Security Act, as some members of his WP had been subject to. It was also a matter of personal pride — given the ignominy of entering Parliament "by the grace of the government" — that seemed to be among the reasons behind Jeyaretnam's rejection of the scheme.

Jeyaretnam also declared his party would not accept any offers of an NCMP seat, a position also shared by other opposition leaders including Chiam See Tong, then of the Singapore Democratic Party (SDP) — although Jeyaretnam would later renege on his pledge in 1997 when he himself was offered an NCMP seat.

1984–5 — No takers for the NCMP position

The 1984 General Election saw a new wave of support for the opposition. Two opposition MPs — Jeyaretnam and Chiam — were elected, which meant that one NCMP seat would be offered to the opposition.

M.P.D. Nair of the WP, who became the 'best loser' from among the opposition with 48.8% of the vote he garnered in Jalan Kayu, became the first person to be offered an NCMP position. A veteran in Singapore politics who briefly served as a minister in 1959 in the Singapore People Alliance government of Lim Yew Hock, he was said to have been eager to accept the seat, but was upset when his party instructed him to decline it.[3] The Central Executive Committee (CEC) of the WP voted against accepting the seat, citing its firm position of opposing the NCMP scheme on a matter of principle.

The seat was then offered to the losing opposition candidate with the next highest vote share in the constituency he contested — Tan Chee Kien, the chairman of the Singapore United Front (SUF), who garnered 47.7% in Kaki Bukit. After polling night, Tan was quick to decline any offer of an NCMP seat in the name of preserving a coherent opposition stance on the issue,[4] though the SUF vacillated. The CEC of the SUF ultimately voted against Tan accepting the seat, though not without a dramatic twist — Seow Khee Leng, the SUF secretary-general, made a police report after thugs had threaten to harm his family and him if the CEC of the SUF did not allow Tan to take up the NCMP seat.[5]

Parliament then decided not to make further offers under the NCMP scheme. There were thus no NCMPs in the Parliament of 1985 to 1988, while Jeyaretnam and Chiam were the only two elected opposition MPs.

1988–9 — Lee Siew Choh becomes the first NCMP

The 1988 General Election was noted for the keenly contested fight between the PAP and the WP teams in Eunos GRC, the latter of which featured Francis Seow, the former solicitor-general, and Lee Siew Choh, the erstwhile leader of the Barisan Sosialis which merged with the WP shortly before the election. The WP team was within one percentage point of winning the GRC.

As Chiam of the SDP was the only elected opposition candidate of that election, two NCMP offers were made, to the WP team that contested Eunos. In a reversal of the WP's position on the NCMP scheme, its CEC voted to allow Seow and Lee to take up the NCMP seats. To explain their volte-face, the speculation had been that the WP leaders were wary of letting the SDP dominate opposition politics, because if the WP were to decline the NCMP seats, the next two best performing opposition losing candidates were from the SDP. On the eve of the 1988 election, when there was a flurry of party mergers following talks within the opposition, the WP and SDP did not see eye-to-eye on a number of issues.[6]

Francis Seow, however, was ultimately disqualified from taking the seat even before that Parliament session opened. Having been convicted of tax evasion offences between polling day and the opening of Parliament, Seow claimed he was denied his NCMP seat.[7] The government made no further offers of NCMP seats, and Lee Siew Choh thus became the first NCMP in Singapore, and the only NCMP in Parliament from 1989 to 1991.

That represented Lee's return to Parliament, 25 years after he boycotted the House in protest of Singapore's declaration of independence, which he claimed that Singaporeans did not want.

During his tenure as the inaugural holder of the NCMP position, Lee Siew Choh spoke on a wide range of issues in Parliament. This notably included the Elected Presidency scheme, to which he signalled the WP's intended boycott of Singapore's first direct elections for the presidency, due to their misgivings about the system of presidential candidates would be selected, as well as old issues such as the abolition of the Internal Security Act. He was also memorably outspoken about the issue of caning as a punishment for non-violent crimes, as well as on the introduction of the Certificate of Entitlement scheme for car ownership in Singapore. He made headlines and, in the Parliament chamber, cut a figure who was "conspicuous in his opposition."[8] This was partly because the positions he took were frequently more aggressive towards the government than that of Chiam, the only other opposition MP — though it was arguable how much of that public attention he received translated into votes.

Characterised as "the longest campaigning war-horse against the Government", and a "never-say-die" critic who was perceived to oppose just about anything the PAP government stood for,[9] Lee Siew Choh would likely have performed exactly as he did in the Parliament of 1989 to 1991, had he entered the house as a fully elected MP rather than an NCMP. Likewise, the government sought ways to treat him as a fully elected MP would have been, notably inviting him to join Lee Kuan Yew's delegation on a key tour of China in 1990 — the first such visit after Singapore officially recognised the People's Republic of China that year. (Chiam, the fully elected opposition MP of that Parliament, was similarly invited to join the delegation, but was prevented from doing so as he was unwell.)

As the inaugural holder of the NCMP position, Lee found himself having to test the boundaries of the role. He quickly learnt, for instance, that the Housing and Development Board would not allow him to set up an office in Eunos GRC which he contested in 1988, because he was not deemed to represent any constituency.[10] Adding to the complication was that Lee was not the leader of the party he represented as the NCMP. That role was held by Jeyaretnam who was not in Parliament then.

When speaking on the Elected Presidency Bill, for which he conveyed the WP's intended boycott of the presidential elections, Lee was mocked by the PAP leaders for seemingly trying to distance himself from the views of that of his party chief.[11]

1991 — The opposition sweeps four seats; no NCMP offers made

Lee contested in Eunos GRC again at the following general election in 1991, but did not match his own results in 1988 — in spite of a growing wave of support for the opposition that left the PAP with its lowest share of the popular vote hitherto. Lee fell out with Jeyaretnam and left the WP in 1993.[12]

By the 1991 General Election, the momentum was very much with the SDP among the opposition camp. They took three seats, and Chiam, as SDP chief, was recognised by the government as the "unofficial leader of the opposition". A fourth opposition candidate, Low Thia Khiang of the WP, won Hougang. As the number of opposition MPs duly elected exceeded the threshold of three as set, no offers of NCMP seats were made. This remains the only general election to date which did not see any NCMP seat being offered.

1997 — Jeyaretnam reneges on his position regarding NCMPs

After the period of his disqualification from elections lapsed, Jeyaretnam contested in Cheng San GRC, which became the best performing opposition team in the 1997 General Election. With the reelection of Chiam in Potong Pasir and Low in Hougang, one offer of an NCMP seat was made to the WP's Cheng San team.

WP members were apparently split between those supporting Jeyaretnam in taking up the offer — because they felt that "age [was] catching up" with the then 71-year-old WP chief — and those who believed he ought to stick to his stand on the NCMP scheme.[13]

Jeyaretnam ultimately decided to accept the NCMP offer. He explained that it was a chance to represent the 45% of Cheng San residents who had voted for the WP, whom he said had been subjected to the threats of the PAP of withholding national infrastructure from the constituency if it voted for the WP. Jeyaretnam also cited the precedent set by his party in endorsing Francis Seow and Lee Siew Choh for the NCMP seats offered to them in 1988.[14] Wong Kan Seng, as Leader of the House, chided Jeyaretnam for entering Parliament "by the grace of the government" — the very words Jeyaretnam had used in 1984 when criticising the NCMP scheme. Then PAP MP Tan Cheng Bock remarked that he was "surprised. I thought [Jeyaretnam] was a man of principle." Years later when the Progress Singapore Party team for West Coast GRC team — of which Tan was a part after he left the PAP — was offered two NCMP seats in 2020, Tan personally declined the seat.

The NCMP scheme, 1989–2001: Boon or bane for the opposition?

The first two NCMPs — Lee Siew Choh and J. B. Jeyaretnam — were political veterans when they were offered NCMP seats. Their parliamentary stints were the swan song of their long political careers, rather than heralding any new political agenda. The media ridiculed Lee as "an old gramophone record out of sync with the times".[15] Jeyaretnam even declared, when reentering Parliament in 1997, that "I shall continue as I did in 1981 to '86."[16] They were also known to give long speeches — Lee Siew Choh having infamously chalked up a record 7.5 hours in Parliament on a debate on merger with Malaysia, in an apparent filibustering attempt, before parliamentary rules were revised to preclude that possibility ever again. One does wonder if the PAP leaders regretted devising the NCMP scheme, only for their old nemeses to take up the role.[17]

The NCMP scheme therefore offered Lee and Jeyaretnam — as individuals — a final chance to make a dent in Parliament for the opposition. It did crucially keep the WP in the game, especially at a time when law suits brought by the PAP leaders against Jeyaretnam threatened to extinguish his party altogether by 2001. In so doing, it kept the WP relevant for long enough to continue attracting candidates whom they could field. It proved, however, insufficient for reviving the party's fortunes.

Since then, every single NCMP has been new to Parliament when they were offered the role. An assessment of those subsequent NCMPs, and what the NCMP role had done for them, is covered in Ng Wai Mun's chapter in this book.

2001–11 — 'Constructive opposition politics' and the rise of a new WP

Steve Chia, the secretary-general of the National Solidarity Party which contested the 2001 General Election under the banner of the Singapore Democratic Alliance, became the sole NCMP in that Parliament. At about the same time, the WP was undergoing a leadership transition from Jeyaretnam to Low Thia Khiang who was to bring about a less 'confrontational' approach to opposition politics. Sylvia Lim was integral to the WP's revamp, and became an NCMP from the WP's Aljunied GRC team in the 2006 General Election.

In April 2010, Parliament passed amendments to the Constitution and the Parliamentary Elections Act to increase the maximum number of NCMPs to nine. Wong Kan Seng, who tabled the bill as the then Deputy Prime Minister, offered the rationale that "As we mature as a society and our citizens become better educated and informed, we see a growing desire among Singaporeans to follow and express views on important national matters."[18]

Sylvia Lim went on to become the first NCMP to be successfully elected to Parliament at the next General Election in 2011, as part of the Aljunied team that made history as the first opposition candidates to capture a GRC.

As the WP won Hougang Single Member Constituency (SMC) and the five-member GRC of Aljunied, three NCMP offers were made.

The best losing opposition candidate in 2011 was Lina Chiam of the Singapore People's Party (SPP), who contested Potong Pasir SMC and lost by a razor thin margin of 114 votes. This was followed by an NCMP offer made to the WP's Yee Jenn Jong, who was just 388 votes short of winning Joo Chiat SMC. The next and final offer of an NCMP seat was made to the WP team which contested the five-member East Coast GRC. The question of who from the team would take up the NCMP seat caused a furore in the WP.

Eric Tan, the leader of the GRC team who also chaired the WP's Eastern Area Committee, was the presumptive taker of that final NCMP offer. At a meeting of the WP's CEC, however, the majority of its CEC members voted instead for Gerald Giam — another candidate in the WP's East Coast GRC team who was 20 years Tan's junior — to take up the NCMP seat, apparently on the basis of "party renewal".[19] Tan resigned from the WP because he felt betrayed. According to him, WP chief Low had promised to nominate him to be an NCMP shortly before the elections.[20]

"I felt betrayed by Low as he promised to support me for the NCMP position before the elections. Low told me to work hard and win the NCMP seat in East Coast GRC for the party. I knew it was a tall order as Chiam [See Tong's SPP team] at Bishan-Toa Payoh GRC was a formidable competitor for that seat. Low assured me that being Secretary-General, the CEC would likely support his recommendation. When I produced the results, Low broke his word. He told the CEC and I that he had changed his mind, as he did not expect only one offer of an NCMP seat to be made to our East Coast GRC team.

"I resigned from the party as I found Low's explanation unacceptable due to my concerns about integrity. I told the press I felt betrayed by Low, but the press did not report the first part — they gave the public the impression that I felt betrayed just because the party did not choose me to be NCMP."

— Eric Tan[21]

2015–6 — Furore as Lee Li Lian's NCMP seat is "transferred"

In the 2015 General Election, Lee Li Lian emerged as the best losing opposition candidate, when she garnered 48.2% in Punggol East SMC, to which she was elected in a by-election two years earlier. Given that there were only five opposition MPs elected, the Elections Department announced she was elected as an NCMP. However, Lee was quick to decline the offer on polling night, citing reasons of child care. The next two best losing opposition candidates were also from the WP — Dennis Tan, who contested Fengshan SMC, and Leon Perera, from the WP's team which contested East Coast GRC.

The WP called for Lee's NCMP offer to be "transferred" to Daniel Goh, the next best losing opposition candidate who was also from their East Coast GRC team. They moved a motion in Parliament to facilitate that "transfer", given that the Parliamentary Elections Act was silent on such a manoeuvre. This met with brickbats from the PAP, whose leaders accused the WP of "trying to game the system" in order to "showcase" its party talents — in this case, Daniel Goh. They also criticised WP chief Low, who had colourfully described NCMPs as "duckweeds" — parliamentarians with no roots in a constituency — and yet the WP had chosen to accept the NCMP offers for a number of general elections by now.

Low offered a two-pronged explanation. He said the NCMP scheme could be used inappropriately to "vent emotions in a show, but with no real consequence", though he also recognised "Parliament is a forum to discuss issues", and that "having one more NCMP will contribute to the debate and possibly better policy outcomes."

Ultimately, the PAP majority in Parliament voted to extend the offer of an NCMP seat to Daniel Goh, though not without amending the WP's original motion to say that Parliament

> Regrets that Ms Lee Li Lian, having stood as a Workers' Party candidate and received the highest vote share among all losing candidates, has now decided to give up her NCMP seat to another candidate from her party with a lower vote share, contrary to the expressed will of the voters. And that the WP supports this political manoeuvre to take full advantage of the NCMP seat, even as its secretary-general criticises NCMPs as just duckweed on the water of the pond.

In protest at the slight, all WP MPs abstained on the final vote on the amended motion.

In November 2016, Parliament passed constitutional amendments which raised the maximum number of NCMPs from nine to 12. In a reversal of the principle of the NCMP scheme as laid down by Lee Kuan Yew in 1984, NCMPs were now being granted full voting rights as MPs. In explaining his rationale when first introducing the changes in early 2016, Prime Minister Lee Hsien Loong said that "if we accept that NCMPs have as much of a mandate from voters to be in the House as constituency Members of Parliament... I will [make] the case that they should not only be allowed to speak, but to vote."[22]

2020 — Two NCMPs from the PSP

The Progress Singapore Party (PSP) — a new political party led by former PAP backbencher Tan Cheng Bock, making its maiden outing in the 2020 General Election — fielded its star team in the five-member West Coast GRC, which then emerged as that election's best losing opposition candidates with 48.3% of the vote. Two offers of NCMP seats were made to the PSP's West Coast GRC team, as the WP had won 10 seats.

While being the face of the fledgling party to most Singaporeans, Tan declined to take up an NCMP seat given his consistent stance against the scheme. Instead, the CEC of the PSP voted for Leong Mun Wai and Hazel Poa to take up the two NCMP seats. During the campaign, Leong had publicly rejected taking up an NCMP position if offered, but ultimately deferred to Tan as the party's secretary-general.[23]

In a highly unusual move, Leong and Poa stepped down from the leadership positions they held on the party's CEC. They were assistant secretary-general and vice-chairman respectively, and thus among the most senior of the party leadership. The reason proffered by the party was that they were "relieved of internal party responsibilities so that they can focus on their parliamentary duties as NCMPs"[24] — which did not explain how parliamentarians from other parties, including the PAP and the WP, have managed to retain their internal party responsibilities while also playing an active role in Parliament.

Almost from the outset, Leong garnered widespread attention in the media for his "aggressive" and "confrontational" questioning of the government, which earned the ire of the PAP leaders for allegedly peddling misinformation. Leong served as the PSP's secretary-general from 2023 to 2024, after which Poa took over the position and has served to date.

Why did PSP's NCMPs step down from leadership roles?

"Dr Tan Cheng Bock [as leader of the PSP] had convinced us to just concentrate on Parliament initially, because there was going to be a lot of work. And we do not have a legislative assistant. Everything is done by ourselves."

— Leong Mun Wai[25]

"It was not meant to be permanent. It was because we were so new and had very little support. And we did not have current MPs to guide us along."

— Hazel Poa[26]

Conclusion — confusion and ambiguities over a uniquely Singaporean innovation?

The NCMP scheme is a uniquely Singaporean innovation, notwithstanding the reference its creators made to the Mauritius example. It has added a little element of political theatrics and twists in what is otherwise a straight-forward first-past-the-post, Westminster electoral system.

But as this overview of the scheme's history has shown, the operation of the NCMP scheme over the years has thrown up some questions as to whether there has been a consistent purpose which it was meant to serve. Consider just for instance:

— The Parliamentary Elections Act does not lay down the number of alternative offers of NCMP positions that must be made, if there are NCMPs who decline each offer made to them. Rather, it gives Parliament — in effect, the government of the day, since it is they who will carry the majority in any parliamentary resolution — broad latitude in deciding how many alternative offers are made, if at all. This has led to incidents such as the tussle between the government and the WP over the "transfer" of Lee Li Lian's NCMP seat to Daniel Goh in 2016. The government weaponised the issue against the WP, pointing out in quite combative language the contradiction of the WP's criticism of the NCMP scheme while continuing to accept the NCMP offers themselves.

There is nothing wrong with what is essentially a political — as opposed to a codified — resolution to the question of how many alternative NCMP offers are to be made. However, if the government's raison d'etre for the NCMP scheme is to guarantee the electorate a minimum number of opposition members in Parliament, then the spirit in which the scheme has been implemented has not matched the stated guarantee.

— There is some arbitrariness as to which candidate or candidates from a GRC team are to accept the NCMP seats offered to the team. No doubt the Parliamentary Elections Act is clear that the candidates in that GRC team must decide among themselves who is to accept the NCMP seat, and that no more than two offers of NCMP seats may be made to each GRC team. In practice, the candidates in such a situation have deferred to the CEC of their party to make the decision. This effectively led to a standoff in 2011 between Eric Tan, the presumed leader of the WP's East Coast GRC team, and the CEC of the WP, whose preferred choice was for Gerald Giam from the team to take up the NCMP seat. There is nothing to suggest that the government had designed the scheme to engineer such instances of intra-opposition strife. However, this is an instance of the government's innovation of the NCMP scheme jarring with its other innovation of the GRC system (which was introduced four years after the NCMP scheme) — with the result of diminishing the principles of democratic representation and responsibility which the PAP no doubt seeks to uphold. Note for instance the parliamentary debate in 2016 over the issue of the NCMP seat "transfer" from Lee Li Lian to Daniel Goh, during which Chan Chun Sing, then Minister in the Prime Minister's Office, castigated Lee Li Lian for rejecting the NCMP seat and, by extension, abdicating "her responsibility to her voters and Singapore".[27] But how do these same strict principles apply to members of a GRC team, when clearly not every candidate on the team will have a chance of accepting the offer of an NCMP position, when it is put to their team?

— There appears to be some confusion — or inconsistency — as to what the raison d'être of the NCMP scheme is, even among the PAP which created the scheme. In 2016, Chan Chun Sing accused the WP of abusing the NCMP scheme to "showcase" their "party talents" — in this case, by "manoeuvring" to "transfer" the NCMP seat from Lee Li Lian to Daniel Goh — rather than for the more noble purpose of "[serving] Singapore and Singaporeans." While Chan was taking issue with the WP's "transfer" of the NCMP seat between WP candidates, the thrust of Chan's argument was at odds with the stated aims of the NCMP scheme made by earlier PAP leaders such as Goh Chok Tong, who was on the record for saying that an NCMP could establish himself if he did well in Parliament, and that this would help attract other good candidates to join his political party[28] — in other words, the opposition could use the NCMP scheme to "showcase" its "party talents". Lee Kuan Yew also had no qualms saying that one of the benefits of having an opposition in Parliament, such as through the NCMP scheme, was to "[sharpen] the debating skills" of younger PAP ministers and MPs.[29]

Again, there is nothing to suggest that the government had designed the NCMP scheme to trap the opposition in these ways. But it does beg the question — what exactly is the purpose of the NCMP scheme?

3

Evolution of the NCMP Scheme
With Reflections by Politicians and Observers

Yee Jenn Jong

When the Non-Constituency Member of Parliament (NCMP) scheme was first created in August 1984, it provided for only up to three NCMPs.[1] That was at a time when there was one elected opposition MP — J. B. Jeyaretnam. The General Election of December 1984 saw two opposition MPs being elected. The maximum number of NCMPs was raised to nine in 2010.[2] At that time, there were only two elected opposition MPs — Chiam See Tong and Low Thia Khiang, with Sylvia Lim being the sole NCMP. Interestingly, at the following general election in 2011, the opposition won a then record high of six seats, including the capture of a Group Representation Constituency (GRC) for the first time. That resulted in three NCMPs entering Parliament. After the subsequent change of the scheme to increase the number of NCMPs to up to 12 in 2016,[3] the opposition made yet another breakthrough of a second GRC in the following 2020 General Election, hence winning a total of 10 seats. That resulted in just two NCMPs being appointed.

In this chapter, we look at the political climate during the period of these changes, examining the debate and ground reactions then. Who benefitted from these changes — was it the People's Action Party (PAP) or the opposition?

The initial years — when there were just three

The origin of the scheme and the surrounding political climate and debates then have been covered in detail in Chapter 2. In the 1984 General Election, just after the introduction of the scheme, the PAP saw the biggest ever vote swing against it, a 12.9% dip in support to 64.8%. This was against a backdrop of various contributing factors which included the unpopular Graduate Mothers' Scheme and the raising of the age for Central Provident Fund withdrawal. It was also the passing of the baton from the first to the second generation of PAP leaders.

During that general election, opposition candidates performed better amid the national swing against the PAP. Jeyaretnam of the Workers' Party (WP) won with a bigger margin and Chiam of the Singapore Democratic Party (SDP) won on his fourth electoral attempt with a convincing 60.28%. The NCMP position was offered to M.P.D. Nair of the WP who scored a very credible 48.78%. Nair rejected the seat, which was then offered to Tan Chee Kien of the Singapore United Front (SUF) who also had a sizable 47.72% of the votes. Tan did not accept as well and no further seats were offered.

The 1984 General Election was the first time the NCMP scheme came into play and understandably, it was used extensively by the PAP during campaigning to assure voters that they could safely vote for the PAP and yet have opposition representatives in Parliament. That did not seem to work given the massive 12.9% national swing against the ruling party. Then Prime Minister Lee Kuan Yew had expressed surprise that the swing against the PAP was bigger than he had expected. It was the first time since Independence that the PAP received less than 70% of the overall votes.[4]

Across the board, opposition parties gained vote shares in seats they had contested. Even with the assurance that there would be elected opposition voices in Parliament through the NCMP scheme, many had voted for the opposition, especially those who represented the more established parties and possessed credible professional qualifications. Table 1 shows opposition candidates who received over 40% of the vote share for their respective constituencies.

In the next general election on 3 September 1988, the PAP vote share declined slightly to 63.1%. That GE saw the introduction of the GRC scheme. There were 13 GRCs comprising three members each and 42 Single Member Constituencies (SMCs). The Barisan Sosialis and the SUF had merged with the WP. Jeyaretnam had to vacate his Anson SMC seat due to an earlier conviction over falsified party accounts and was barred from the general election. Only Chiam retained his seat. In four GRCs and nine SMCs, the leading opposition teams polled above 40%.

Two NCMP positions were offered to Francis Seow and Dr Lee Siew Choh of the WP for garnering 49.1% votes share in Eunos GRC. Just before the election, Seow was detained without trial under the Internal Security Act. He then left Singapore after release to seek medical treatment and never returned to face trial for alleged tax evasion. Seow was disqualified from taking up the position. Lee became Singapore's

Table 1: Electoral Performance of Opposition Candidates in the 1984 General Election

SN	Candidate	Party	Constituency	Vote %
1	M.P.D. Nair	WP	Jalan Kayu	48.78
2	Tan Chee Kien	SUF	Kaki Bukit	47.72
3	Wong Hong Toy	WP	Radin Mas	46.22
4	Rajaratnam Murugason	WP	Telok Blangah	44.98
5	Chan Keng Sieng	WP	Chua Chu Kang	44.35
6	Jufrie Mahmood	WP	Kg Kembangan	44.29
7	Ling How Doong	SDP	Chong Boon	43.98
8	Lee Siew Choh	Barisan Sosialis	Boon Teck	43.84
9	Seow Khee Leng	SUF	Kg Chai Chee	42.84
10	Royston George Scharenguivel	WP	Kolam Ayer	42.09
11	Soon Kia Seng	SDP	Changkat	41.44
12	Peter Chua Chwee Huat	WP	Delta	41.28
13	Chon Koon Cheong	WP	Henderson	41.20

Source: https://www.eld.gov.sg/elections_past_parliamentary1984.html

first NCMP, making his return to Parliament 25 years after being legislator for the PAP and then for Barisan Sosialis.

The following general elections in 1991 was a landmark for the opposition. Four seats were lost to the opposition — Chiam retained Potong Pasir SMC, Low Thia Khiang, Ling How Doong and Cheo Chai Chen won Hougang SMC, Bukit Gombak SMC and Nee Soon Central SMC, respectively. That made the SDP as the largest opposition party with three seats followed by the WP with one. This remained the only general election so far since the introduction of the NCMP scheme that no NCMP positions were offered as the number of opposition candidates elected exceeded the number reserved for opposition legislators. The PAP received its lowest ever vote share from contested seats since

Independence, dropping to 60.97%, which marked the third consecutive decline in its vote share.

One key factor in that general election was the by-election strategy. The opposition collaborated and contested less than 50% of available seats, thereby returning the PAP to power on Nomination Day. That was intended to let voters vote at ease knowing that there would be no freak election outcome resulting in the PAP losing power. It neutralised one of the key assurances provided for in the NCMP scheme that voters could choose the PAP to prevent a freak electoral result while still having opposition voices in Parliament.

In the subsequent three general elections held in 1997, 2001 and 2006, the opposition had only two MPs elected — Chiam and Low. The NCMP positions for those parliamentary terms went to J.B Jeyaretnam, Steve Chia and Sylvia Lim, respectively. PAP's vote shares in these GEs were 64.98% (1997), 75.29% (2001) and 66.6% (2006). The opposition were neither able to repeat the by-election strategy of 1991 nor pose a significant threat to the PAP in those general elections.

Then it became nine

In July 2010, the Constitution was amended to provide automatically for nine opposition members in Parliament.[5] According to the government, the key reasons for the changes were[6]:

1. To cater to citizens who have become better educated and informed, with a growing desire to see greater diversity of views on issues discussed and debated in Parliament;
2. To acknowledge that the four NCMPs Parliament had since the start of the scheme had fulfilled the government's original intent

for it, and it was time to increase the allocation to be the same as that for NMPs (nine).

The amendment to the Constitution was opposed by the WP (represented by Low; Lim spoke extensively during the debate to oppose but was not able to vote as an NCMP) and the Singapore Democratic Alliance (represented by Chiam).

The 2011 General Election that followed was a landmark one. All the then elected opposition MPs, Chiam and Low vacated their SMC seats to contest in Bishan-Toa Payoh GRC and Aljunied GRC, respectively. It created a reverse freak election effect — that there could be a total wipeout of elected opposition MPs. Low declared that he would reject the NCMP seat if he were offered an NCMP seat as one of the best performing opposition candidates (this was similar to the position he had stated in Parliament during the 2010 debate on the constitutional amendments on the NCMP scheme). Chiam also declared in a doorstop interview during the campaigning that he was "not interested in the NCMP position".[7]

The move by the only two then opposition MPs to leave their 'safe' SMCs they had long held, together with better qualified opposition candidates, as well as various national issues creating unhappiness amongst electorates[8] saw the historical first of the loss of a GRC to the opposition. The 'GRC fortress' of the PAP which came into effect in the 1988 General Election, had finally been breached by the WP in Aljunied GRC. Six opposition candidates from the WP were elected — five from Aljunied GRC and one from Hougang SMC.

After sharply reversing their decline in vote share in the 1997 General Election, the PAP also suffered a significant drop of 6.46% in popular votes to 60.14%, its lowest since Independence.

An ageing Chiam, who was also physically weakened by an earlier stroke in 2008, failed in his bid for Bishan-Toa Payoh GRC. His wife, Lina Chiam of his Singapore People's Party (SPP), also failed to defend his previous stronghold in Potong Pasir SMC, as she lost to a PAP candidate by razor-thin margin. With six elected opposition MPs, the three NCMP positions went to Lina Chiam of the SPP and Gerald Giam and Yee Jenn Jong of the WP.

Did the increase in the number of NCMP seats have any effect on the voting? Looking at the result which saw an erosion in the ruling party's vote share and the highest number of elected seats for the opposition since Independence, it did not seem to benefit the PAP. Other factors appeared to have negated the benefit to the ruling party of assuring the voters that they could still have the PAP government and opposition voices in Parliament. The reverse fear of a total opposition wipeout and the potential loss of a respected opposition parliamentarian like Low seemed to weigh heavily on voters' minds, particularly amongst Aljunied and Hougang voters. Threats made against voters by the PAP in hotly contested Aljunied also appeared to have backfired.

As with all general elections before this, the issue of NCMPs continued to be a topic used by both the PAP and the opposition candidates in 2011. During a television forum, Prime Minister Lee Hsien Loong refuted claims that NCMPs were not a "real opposition" as they could speak in Parliament and that the scheme acknowledged both "the desire among Singaporeans for alternative voices and the need for an opposition to represent the diverse views in society".[9]

As an active campaigner in the 2011 General Election and an NCMP as a result of that general election, this author thinks that the NCMP scheme had a minimal effect on how voters cast their vote in that landmark poll. Even with the increase in the number of NCMP seats, the excitement of the scheme only happened after the polling results where all eyes would be on whether opposition candidates would be NCMPs and if so, who would be qualified to be NCMPs by being the 'best losers'. This author did not come across any voter asking him about this matter during campaigning. The interactions appeared more on whether his party or himself would be the appropriate choice to represent them as a fully elected representative. The author acknowledges that the NCMP scheme could have an effect of encouraging higher participation in a general election by opposition candidates as there was an increased chance for opposition candidates to be in Parliament to have the platform to prove themselves. This was however the last thing on my mind as I was focused on campaigning to be a fully elected legislator. The 2011 General Election saw all seats, save for Tanjong Pagar GRC, being contested. It was the most contested general election since Independence, surpassed only by the subsequent general elections in 2015 and 2020 where all seats were contested.

The arrangement for a maximum of nine NCMPs continued in the 2015 General Election. The WP retained Hougang SMC and just held on to the Aljunied GRC seats by less than 1% of the popular vote. It was a big win for the ruling PAP. Singapore's highly respected founding father, Lee Kuan Yew had passed away in February of that year and it was also the 50th anniversary of Singapore's Independence. With huge publicity from the 50th anniversary and the immense gratitude that Singaporeans had for the late Lee, there was a massive 9.72% vote swing back to the PAP. The Punggol East SMC, which was won by Lee Li Lian of the WP in the 2013 by-election was regained by the PAP. The resulting three NCMP seats were all offered to the WP — to Lee Li Lian who contested in Punggol East SMC, Dennis Tan who stood in Fengshan SMC and

Leon Perera who was part of the opposition party's East Coast GRC team. Lee Li Lian rejected the seat and it was eventually filled by Associate Professor Daniel Goh of the East Coast GRC team.

The 2015 General Election saw a huge drop in vote shares for all opposition political parties. In particular, the smaller parties fared a lot worse, with some dropping 15–20% in the same seats where the same party had contested in the previous general election. The result saw a two-party parliament, with 83 seats taken by the PAP and six elected and three NCMP seats by the WP.

And now there are twelve

A year after GE2015, the ruling party proposed to increase the maximum number of NCMPs to 12 and also to give NCMPs the same voting and speaking rights in Parliament as the elected MPs. The increase to 12 was formalised in 2019, a year before the 2020 General Election.

The PAP's main arguments for the increase were[10]:

1. To recognise that NCMPs have as much of a mandate from voters as constituency MPs;
2. To cater for the electorate's desire for an opposition voice in Parliament in view that the opposition had garnered at least 30% support in past elections; hence an increase to 12 opposition MPs inclusive of NCMPs in a 100-member House was reasonable.

The changes were opposed by the WP, then the only opposition party in Parliament. The WP repeated its call for greater changes to the political system for a more level playing field.

NCMPs: A distraction for the electorate?

"The PAP is hoping that a system with more NCMPs will distract the electorate from the need to vote in elected MPs from alternative parties. This is to entrench the Parliament supermajority of the PAP. We need more than just NCMPs to check the Government. We need a good political system whereby a check and balance mechanism on the Government can be implemented through a fair and competitive election process.

"When the voters vote for opposition candidates and the opposition candidates successfully become fully elected Members of Parliament, they will then be able to enter Parliament with the full mandate of the voters and can then be said to truly represent the constituencies who voted them into Parliament. A NCMP does not represent any constituency. The point is, it is the fear of losing elected seats in General Elections that compels the PAP to take the pleas of the people seriously."

— Dennis Tan, then an NCMP, in a Mandarin speech during the debate on the Constitution Amendment on NCMPs, 8 November 2016

Enhancing our existing parliamentary democracy

"Rather than focus on the NCMP scheme as the solution to Singaporeans' desire for alternative voices, we should enhance our existing Parliamentary democracy to make it truly contestable.

"Delink the People's Association from the ruling party. Reform the regulation of the media to allow for regulated but free competition in broadsheet newspapers, TV and radio. Set electoral boundaries transparently and consultatively. Educate every voter aggressively from the classroom onwards that their votes are in fact secret. Many voters still do not believe this.

"Madam, I would like to conclude with a single, very simple question to the Government. With this amendment to the NCMP scheme, is it your goal that your party wins 100% of elected seats in Parliament? This is not a question about whether the people will ultimately determine the outcome of elections and not the Government and not the PAP. I know they will and I do not need to be told that. It is a question about your goal as a ruling party for the next General Election."

— Leon Perera, then an NCMP, in a Mandarin speech during the debate on the Constitution Amendment on NCMPs, 9 November 2016

The 2020 General Election was also a 'Covid-19' General Election, with campaigning severely restricted due to the ongoing pandemic and the absence of any public rallies. It was a general election that should have benefitted the ruling party given the massive support package of nearly S$100 billion to save jobs. With the general fear amongst the electorate at a time of global crisis, the PAP touted its steady records for steering Singapore out of previous crises. There was also the increased guarantee now of 12 opposition representatives through the NCMP scheme.

Given the increase in the number of available NCMP positions, it was not surprising that the PAP brought the issue up several times during campaigning. The opposition, notably the WP which had the highest share of the NCMP positions historically and all of the NCMPs in the 2015–2020 Parliament term, also argued fervently why the scheme did not provide for the real competition and opposition that Singapore needed. The general election also saw a new party, the Progress Singapore Party (PSP) founded by former seven-time PAP MP Dr Tan Cheng Bock who also very narrowly lost out by 0.57% in the 2011 Presidential Election and was not able to contest in the subsequent presidential election in 2017 due to late changes to the rules for the contest.[11] He announced during campaigning that he would reject the NCMP seat if it were offered to him.

The 2020 General Election saw the PAP losing another GRC to the WP. The incumbents in Sengkang GRC were defeated by a young WP team which did not have any experienced legislators and had little electoral experience with only He Ting Ru participating in the 2015 General Election.

The PSP had fielded 24 candidates — the largest slate among opposition parties. The WP only contested in 20 seats. With 10 elected seats going to the WP, the resulting two NCMP seats were offered to the PSP, which went to Leong Mun Wai and Hazel Poa. True to his words, Dr Tan did not take up the position though he was eligible, after leading his West Coast GRC team to a best performing result among unsuccessful opposition candidates.

The increase in the maximum number of NCMPs did not seem to benefit the PAP again. Other issues such as the handling of the pandemic and the increased presence of credible opposition candidates had swung the support to the opposition. As with the other two general election campaigns, this author also did not find any interest by voters he had met about the NCMP issue during campaigning.

Views from observers

Was the PAP generous to increase the opposition presence from three to nine and then to 12 progressively over a period of 36 years? After all, the NCMP scheme had been the PAP's invention to allow for opposition presence in Parliament to cater to voters who wish to have more alternative voices. With a weak and fragmented opposition after years of political dominance by the PAP, the opposition candidates had found it hard to enter Parliament with an outright election win. Since the introduction of the scheme in 1984, only once did the number of elected opposition candidates exceed the number of opposition presence that was guaranteed by the PAP.

Prior to 1981, there had been no opposition in Parliament since the 1968 General Election. The PAP had to find ways to involve backbenchers to provide alternative views and debate with Ministers such as assigning backbenchers to government parliamentary committees that would then offer additional views to Ministers. With breakthroughs by the opposition in the 1980s, new electoral innovations came about — first the NCMP scheme, the Town Councils, the GRC and NMP schemes as well as the Elected Presidency.

Did the increase in the maximum number of NCMPs in 2011 and 2020 mean that the PAP was becoming more prepared for opposition voices with the 3G leaders already firmly in control? The politics of the 1980s was more confrontational and acrimonious in nature. From the 2000s, politics became more cordial and constructive. Voters were also more educated and prepared to vote for better opposition candidates and for those in the bigger opposition parties. Was the PAP more prepared for diverse voices especially with 'calmer' opposition voices since 2001?

Perhaps it was coincidental and ironic as well that each time the PAP increased the maximum number of NCMPs, it lost more seats. The resulting effect is that there had never been more than three NCMPs in any parliamentary term, despite the maximum number being set at 12 now. Was the PAP anticipating the level of opposition presence the voters wanted and what they were ready to deal with?

We seek the opinions of politicians and political observers for their views on the progressive increase in the maximum number of NCMPs and what that meant in the context of Singapore's political evolution.

Voters still choose the opposition, despite NCMP scheme

"In Singapore, nothing happens by coincidence! But the fact that voters still chose the opposition in large numbers, shows that the opposition benefitted more. I don't know a single voter who has mentioned the NCMP scheme to me when they were discussing voting.

"The NCMP scheme does not exist in a vacuum. It exists alongside other electoral innovations (GRC, NMP, Elected Presidency) and within the broader socio-political context. Voters usually care about other things such as bread-and-butter issues and fairness of the system, rather than whether there are guaranteed NCMPs. Voters also use the elections as a means to express frustrations towards the ruling party, so there is little worry of the scheme being a deterrent (for opposition votes)."

— Assistant Professor Walid Jumblatt Abdullah, School of Social Sciences, Nanyang Technological University

Quality of opposition candidates and political environment at general election matters

Former PAP MP Inderjit Singh (see interview in Chapter 7) cautioned against reading too much into the fact that each time the maximum number of NCMP positions were increased, the opposition had more elected. He believes that it reflected the quality of the slate of candidates by the opposition and the political environment at the time of those elections which did not favour the PAP.

NCMP scheme undermines development of alternative political parties

"The government gradually increasing potential NCMP seats from three to 12 is consistent with the view that the scheme is intended to tell voters that they can still have an opposition in Parliament and vote PAP. If this were not the intent, surely the presence of more fully elected opposition MPs since 2011 would have made it unnecessary to increase NCMP seats. The NCMP scheme acts so as to persuade voters that they can get the undoubted benefits of having an opposition in Parliament while still voting PAP. In so doing, the scheme, together with other Singapore electoral 'innovations', acts to undermine the project to build alternative political parties to provide healthy competition to the PAP and an alternative for when the PAP fails."

— Leon Perera, former NCMP and former MP

No evidence that increase in NCMPs impacted voters' choices

"In both cases, the NCMP numbers were increased via constitutional amendments forwarded by the PAP before the general elections. One can definitely appreciate and understand the argument that these enhancements were made by the PAP because they recognised the public demanded greater opposition voices in Parliament, and therefore sought to provide for it. Whether the opposition made gains in spite or despite those enhancements is purely speculative. There is also no systematic empirical evidence to evaluate the claim that the increase in NCMP numbers will make it less likely for Singaporeans to consider voting for opposition candidates."

— Assistant Professor Elvin Ong, Department of Political Science, National University of Singapore

4

The NCMP Scheme
Boon or Bane for the Opposition?

Ng Wai Mun

Introduction

Does the Non-Constituency Member of Parliament (NCMP) scheme ultimately help the opposition as a whole, or does it have its limits and work against opposition parties? On the record, political commentators have tended to broadly agree on or propose that both the People's Action Party (PAP) and at least the Workers' Party (WP), the largest and now the most established opposition faction in Parliament, have benefitted from the NCMP scheme, for different reasons, respectively. Most arguments on the pluses of the NCMP scheme, however, have stopped short of providing more details or data on how the scheme works in each of their favour. The political parties themselves have put forth their own narratives about the scheme.

In an attempt to persuade against endowing NCMPs with constitutional voting rights, veteran journalist Bertha Henson, quite interestingly, wrote in a 2020 op-ed[1] that the NCMP scheme is usually good for the PAP before a general election to persuade voters that opposition presence in Parliament is 'guaranteed', while working for opposition parties after the GE, since the best 'losers' can still get into Parliament to speak and raise their profile. Using the timing of when elections are held as a key reference point, Henson's interpretation seeks to explain the psychological effect that such a scheme could have in the mainstream voters' minds, though increasingly, many believe that the NCMP scheme's impact on a more discerning populace is diminishing, and serves merely as a distraction during elections.

In this chapter, we attempt to narrow the discussion to look at a key benchmark: whether the NCMP scheme has contributed towards electoral success — arguably the most important reason one enters politics — both for opposition political parties as well as for the individual seeking office. Has taking up the NCMP seat been definitive in giving an opposition candidate a better shot at getting an elected seat at the following elections? And does it enhance the overall party brand in voters' minds?

Parliamentary presence as a key party resource

What the NCMP scheme provides now are two broad powers for an individual who takes up the seat. Firstly, an NCMP gets to speak in Parliament and participate in debates. From 2020, an NCMP also gets voting rights on constitutional amendments, supply bills and motions of no confidence in the government, that are equal to full MPs. As its name suggests, an NCMP is not rooted to a specific constituency, and hence is not expected to be involved in estate management or serving constituents in a particular locale. One would argue that, given the PAP's dominance in Parliament which restricts the impact when opposition party lawmakers vote against a bill, having parliamentary presence is so far the greatest 'perk' an opposition candidate in Singapore can enjoy if he or she is offered an NCMP seat and takes it up.

Yet one should be cognisant of the fact that since the NCMP scheme was set up in 1984, there are hardly any examples of NCMPs who went on to become fully elected MPs in the constituency they contested in to become NCMPs, with WP's Sylvia Lim being the only exception out of all 12 names (see Table 1). Historically, the first two NCMPs — Lee Siew Choh and J. B. Jeyaretnam, both from WP — were already political

Table 1: Electoral Records of NCMPs

Name of NCMP	Political party	General election contested	Constituency contested	Subsequent general election/s contested (win/loss)	Constituency contested
Steve Chia	Singapore Democratic Alliance	2001	Chua Chu Kang SMC	2006 (Loss); 2011 (Loss); 2020 (Loss)	Chua Chu Kang SMC; Pioneer SMC; Bishan-Toa Payoh GRC
Sylvia Lim	Workers' Party	2006	Aljunied GRC	2011 (Win); 2015 (Win); 2020 (Win)	Aljunied GRC
Lina Chiam	Singapore People's Party	2011	Potong Pasir SMC	2015 (Loss)	Potong Pasir SMC
Yee Jenn Jong	Workers' Party	2011	Joo Chiat SMC	2015 (Loss); 2020 (Loss)	Marine Parade GRC
Gerald Giam	Workers' Party	2011	East Coast GRC	2015 (Loss); 2020 (Win)	East Coast GRC; Aljunied GRC

(*Continued*)

Table 1: *(Continued)*

Name of NCMP	Political party	General election contested	Constituency contested	Subsequent general election/s contested (win/loss)	Constituency contested
Dennis Tan	Workers' Party	2015	Fengshan SMC	2020 (Win)	Hougang SMC
Leon Perera	Workers' Party	2015	East Coast GRC	2020 (Win)	Aljunied GRC
Daniel Goh	Workers' Party	2015	East Coast GRC	—	—

veterans when they were offered NCMP seats. The latter had been relentlessly fighting to re-enter Parliament after his disqualification from his Anson seat in 1986. Their parliamentary stints were the swan song of their long political careers, offering them a final chance to make a dent in Parliament for the opposition. Unfortunately, their time in Parliament did not herald any new political agenda and proved insufficient for reviving the party's fortunes.

Since then, every single NCMP has been new to Parliament when they were offered the role. Steve Chia, the third NCMP, representing the National Solidarity Party (NSP) under an opposition alliance, burst onto the scene in 2001 as a fresh, youthful voice, after a difficult election. Chia was not reelected at the following election for various reasons unconnected to his NCMP role.

After Chia, four out of six of WP's NCMPs would go on to secure electoral success, though three of them — Dennis Tan, Gerald Giam, Leon Perera — who represented the party in the 2020 General Election after serving one stint each as NCMP, were contesting in WP strongholds — and not where they originally contested in — with Giam and Perera placed in the same team in Aljunied GRC alongside party leaders Pritam Singh and Sylvia Lim who have proven track records. It has thus been hard to conclude that their chances of winning had been boosted solely because of their performance as NCMPs.

On a global scale, there is also remarkably scant empirical evidence on the effects that parliamentary presence has on party appeal. What we can be more sure of is that in the Westminster system of first-past-the-post elections, party brand building is essential to opposition parties, more so than personalities. The system is designed in a way to have that effect, argues political commentator Derek da Cunha,[2] and the reality tends to be accentuated in Singapore where there are also multi-seat constituencies. "The starting point for a viable campaign for elected political office is a party ticket with a strong, identifiable brand," he writes.

Broadly, for a political party, beyond institutionalised privileges, entering Parliament provides an opportunity for its members to take part in the policy-making process. Benefits include media visibility, a potential boost in attractiveness for donors, as well as improvements in the organisational know-how of parties. On the other hand, small opposition parties which have repeatedly failed to enter Parliament, even as NCMPs, have reportedly emphasised how onerous it is to sustain the organisational capacity of the party in between elections. If a party's future electoral prospects are perceived by its members as limited, ambitious and skilled political personnel may abandon it. Finally, the appeal of the party suffers, with voters perceiving it as peripheral for policy making.

A 2014 research[3] conducted by overseas researchers — a rare one that provides a data-backed explanation for why entering Parliament might be a key resource for small parties — argues that parliamentary presence is more important for parties in new democracies, where party branding is weak and the need for 'signalling' — to demonstrate that a party has organisational capacity and that its candidates have appeal — is high. Using a data set that covers all post-World War II democracies with a national threshold of representation, its findings reveal that parliamentary presence can help parties win almost two-thirds more votes in comparison with their previous showing. According to the report, "these findings suggest that entering the legislature may be key for broadening the appeal of small parties. While it does not guarantee perennial prosperity, it privileges parties in comparison to their competitors outside Parliament and provides access to valuable resources."

WP's contradictory attitudes towards the NCMP scheme: For lack of a better playing field?

In the Singapore context, given limited understanding of what explains the electoral performance of a small political party — why some are successful in continuously winning seats whereas others wither away — the growth trajectory of the WP, seen alongside its expanded presence and participation in Parliament, is arguably the best (or only) case study we have in scrutinising how the party perceives the effects of parliamentary presence, as well as the potential benefits that the NCMP scheme can bring. This is so especially with the lack of research literature and post-election surveys specifically investigating these questions.

In recent elections, the party's acceptance of NCMP positions despite being fundamentally supportive of the ultimate discontinuation of the NCMP scheme has come under scrutiny. "What does WP really want?"

asks PAP's Heng Swee Keat,[4] now the deputy prime minister of Singapore and a key member of the ruling party's fourth-generation leadership ranks, during the 2020 General Election. "Is the real motive of the Workers' Party to expand, to win more seats in Parliament?" he added, calling for the WP to be upfront during the campaign period if its candidates would accept NCMP seats if offered. Some political observers have gone further to suggest that the WP should now oppose the NCMP scheme and reject the seats as a matter of party policy and principle, now that it has demonstrated that it can win seats outright from the PAP (At the 2020 General Election, it retained Aljunied GRC and Hougang SMC, won the new Sengkang GRC and saw 10 fully elected MPs enter Parliament). It remains to be seen if this is on the minds of WP party leaders.

Growth of WP presence in Parliament against vote share

The WP has consistently expanded its presence in Parliament, but there is so far no direct correlation between the vote share it garners at every election with the size of its presence in Parliament (see Table 2).

Table 2: Workers' Party's Electoral Performance in General Elections from 2001 to 2020

General election contested	No. of parliamentary seats (Full MPs + NCMPs)	Vote share of contested constituencies
2001	1 + 0	36.8%
2006	1 + 1	35.1%
2011	6 + 2	42.6%
2015	6 + 3	36.7%
2020	10 + 0	50.5%

The NCMP scheme at best has a complementary effect towards the WP's electoral success.

What is fascinating and revealing about the WP example is perhaps also how it has possibly deliberated which candidate's name to put forward in some instances, in what some would describe as strategic manoeuvres by the party leadership to enhance the exposure and strengthen name recognition of its pipeline of new talent, though the party has consistently denied that such 'candidate swaps' were intentional.

One most prominent example was in 2016 when WP filed a parliamentary motion for an NCMP seat offered to former Punggol East MP Lee Li Lian to be declared vacant. Lee, who had lost in the single-seat constituency she had won in a by-election, was the best performing among all the losing opposition candidates, but had declared that she would not take up the seat, citing among other reasons her desire to respect the choice of voters who had not voted for her. She added that she "wanted to give other aspiring MPs from WP a chance to speak in Parliament".[5]

It would not be the first time that WP candidates declined an NCMP position. But in filing the motion, WP sought to have sociology don Daniel Goh take up the seat, in a move that it said was supported by the party leadership. Goh was from the party's East Coast GRC team, which received 39.3% of the vote in the 2015 General Election, and was chosen over his other team mates Mohamed Fairoz Shariff and Gerald Giam (the latter already had exposure as a one-stint NCMP); another team mate Leon Perera was already offered the NCMP seat and had accepted. In her Parliament speech,[6] Sylvia Lim, speaking from her experience as an NCMP from 2006 to 2011, argued that if Lee, as an incumbent MP who had served the constituency was just defeated and returned to Parliament as an NCMP, it might be deemed undemocratic. She also highlighted that there is precedent for Parliament to fill an NCMP vacancy.

Goh ended up not contesting in the following general election, citing health reasons.[7] He has since been expelled from WP for disclosing information, allegedly through his social media posts, about the "inner workings" of the opposition party. When he was an NCMP, Goh was actively shadowing Low Thia Khiang in his Bedok Reservoir-Punggol ward in Aljunied GRC until early 2020, when Goh suddenly stepped down from various party positions, citing health reasons. Goh did not contest in the 2020 General Election, and the Bedok Reservoir-Punggol ward was filled by Gerald Giam instead — another former NCMP. This suggests that Goh was originally a key part of the WP's leadership renewal when he was still NCMP. There is otherwise little one can say if his presence in Parliament as an NCMP aided his political career in any way, though the choice that WP made to help Goh enter Parliament was indicative of the weight it accorded the NCMP role. Who it put up as NCMPs following the 2015 General Election could have been especially crucial too, given how the party was badly bruised in the elections, as it nearly lost Aljunied GRC.

Of course, the WP has also made electoral breakthroughs without the direct exposure that the NCMP scheme brings, most notably its win of Sengkang GRC in the 2020 General Election. None of the candidates has parliamentary experience. Voters interviewed post-election said they felt connected to the WP team, although most were new faces, and were sufficiently assured of their pledge to speak up for voters in Parliament. By then, WP was already an established brand and voice in Parliament, with a much clearly articulated ideological profile. What would be worthy to observe is if it indicates that the positive effect that mere parliamentary presence can bring about is diminishing too. As the WP grows in strength, the NCMP scheme would likely also lose its practical relevance for the party.

Best performing NCMP? So what?

Given current political realities that opposition candidates are subjected to, NCMPs, including the best performing ones, are likely not able to secure electoral success just based on their individual merits. For example, two of the former WP NCMPs — Yee Jenn Jong and Dennis Tan — have had single-seat constituencies that they contested in (Joo Chiat and Fengshan respectively) re-delineated and merged into larger GRCs. Yee, who lost Joo Chiat SMC by a mere 388 votes in the 2011 General Election, continued to walk the ground in the constituency, hoping for a second bite of the cherry, but was disappointed to find Joo Chiat SMC being absorbed by neighbouring Marine Parade GRC for the subsequent elections.

Formal and informal tallies by various organisations over the years have also shown that most NCMPs deliver strong performance, quantitative-wise. In explaining WP's victory in Hougang SMC in the 2020 General Election, a book by political observers Bilveer Singh, Walid Jumblatt Abdullah and Felix Tan, said that the WP's Hougang candidate Dennis Tan had "developed a national profile through his active participation in Parliament" and that his stature was "being enhanced by his exemplary performance in Parliament as an NCMP".[8] In three-and-a-half years, Tan had made 49 queries in Parliament, the third most of any MP. Issues he covered included Mass Rapid Transit breakdowns, e-scooter safety, National Service training, climate change and governance. The authors, however, also added that beyond parliamentary presence, Tan needed other factors to win. He had understudied previous

Hougang MP Png Eng Huat since 2016, and had to prove that he was a familiar face in the ward.

For former NCMP Chia who still prides himself for having asked the highest number of questions out of all MPs when he served his NCMP term in the 10th session of Parliament, however, multiple attempts to enter Parliament under different party tickets have so far not been successful.[9] Most recently, in the 2020 General Election, Chia led a five-member team representing Singapore People's Party and lost with 32.77% of the vote.

Observing Progress Singapore Party and Singapore Democratic Party at the next elections

Many opposition politicians now take the view that the NCMP scheme is one that they will have to live with. In separate interviews with the authors of this book, NCMP Hazel Poa from the Progress Singapore Party (PSP) said the scheme can be seen as "a form of affirmative action", whereas Dr Paul Tambyah, chairman of the Singapore Democratic Party (SDP) described it as "palliative care" for a less-than-perfect and floundering democracy.

Poa, who entered Parliament with fellow NCMP Leong Mun Wai, after forcing a 28% swing against the PAP in West Coast GRC, said the scheme gives opposition members an opportunity to be seen and heard, something that most would not have access to in Singapore's media landscape. Poa has been a long-time member of the opposition, and has contested in previous elections on the NSP ticket, including as the party's secretary-general. Her previous tries had been unsuccessful.

So far, the strong performance from PSP in the 2020 General Election has been attributed largely to the personal charisma of former presidential candidate and its chairman Dr Tan Cheng Bock. Some political observers also believe that the performance of the two NCMPs in Parliament could influence the PSP's future electoral performance.[10] What they neglect to say, however, is that the success of these NCMPs as new political actors in scaling their party profile in a positive way could also be contingent upon the dynamics of party competition within Parliament, including how the dominant PAP and WP interacts with them. The PSP NCMPs themselves say that they are unsure if enhanced parliamentary presence could be a double-edged sword, and it is too early to tell what effect it has on electoral success.

This is especially as parties in legislatures have to take a stance on proposed bills, find themselves in the position where they cannot eschew controversial issues, and could suffer negative consequences because of their policy choices. In PSP's case, through parliamentary debates, PAP ministers have repeatedly sought to characterise the party's stance as "anti-foreigner" and "populist", especially as the party often finds itself wading into debates on the government's labour and economic policies. Leong has also received rebukes from the Speaker of Parliament, more recently for striking the rostrum repeatedly while making an argument in the House. It is not known how voters will perceive the NCMP or the party from these parliamentary exchanges.

For the SDP which has not had an NCMP in Parliament before, it would be interesting to see if it would see further improvement in its credibility among voters, especially if it ceases to use extra-institutional channels of protest and instead become active participants in policy making inside legislatures. According to a post-2020 election survey of 4,000 respondents conducted by the Institute of Policy Studies at the Lee Kuan Yew School of Public Policy, the opposition party was the next party after WP to show the greatest improvement in credibility within a decade — from 24% in 2011 to 45% in 2020.[11]

The NCMP scheme was mooted as a safety valve for dissenting views in Parliament, in the event that one party sweeps all seats. As a mechanism, it is meant to be pro-democracy — that is, if democracy is only narrowly defined as ensuring diverse voices in parliamentary debates — and beneficial for both the opposition and the incumbent, so as to ensure that MPs are not deprived of sparring partners in the event no opposition candidates are elected. Yet so far there is no strong conclusive evidence that points to it being the sole factor that has helped the opposition, particularly WP, grow in stature and influence. It might have helped parties which are serious-minded and have the resources and ability to articulate credible alternative policies convince voters that they have electoral viability, but in the absence of data, one can also argue that opposition parties have had to struggle against voters being swayed into voting for the incumbent at elections due to the 'assurance' provided by the NCMP quota, and that some have made electoral progress, not because of the scheme, but despite the scheme.

5

Are NCMPs 'Duckweeds'?
The Roles of the NCMP

Yee Jenn Jong

The roles of the NCMP

In January 2016, the WP had to table a motion in Parliament to get Associate Professor Daniel Goh to fill the Non-Constituency Member of Parliament (NCMP) seat rejected by former Workers' Party (WP) MP Lee Li Lian who had lost narrowly in the 2015 General Election.[1]

During the debate, then WP leader Low Thia Khiang had said that the NCMPs were like "duckweed on the pond", without the benefit of the roots that tied elected MPs to their constituency.[2] Duckweeds are flowering aquatic plants that float on or just beneath the surface of still or slow-moving bodies of fresh water, never fully resting firmly in one place. Low had felt that "there are a lot of things you cannot do as an NCMP [compared to an MP]..." and "as NCMP, you cannot sink roots in that way because you just cannot possibly connect with the residents the way you want."[3]

The use of the word 'duckweed' provided much debate in Parliament with People's Action Party (PAP) parliamentarians decrying WP's position of rejecting the NCMP scheme yet taking up the NCMP positions when offered to them.

Why did Low describe NCMPs as duckweeds? What are the differences between elected MPs and Nominated MPs (NMPs) with NCMPs? Can NCMPs play effective roles in Singapore politics? Has the NCMP scheme met the objectives as initially set up by the PAP? In this chapter, we will examine the roles of NCMPs versus those of MPs and NMPs. We will also look at schemes in other democratic countries that have arrangements that are close to the NCMP scheme.

Differences with elected MPs in Parliament

Prior to the last change to the NCMP scheme in 2017, the rights of NCMPs were the same as those of NMPs, and differentiated from those of elected MPs as presented in Table 1.

Table 1:   Roles and Responsibilities of NCMPs, NMPs and MPs

SN	Area	Specifics
1.	Voting rights	NCMPs can vote on all matters except constitutional amendments, motions to remove the President, motions of no-confidence in the Government, and supply and money Bills. These restrictions were removed for NCMPs in 2017.
2.	Speaking time	An NCMP has a total of 18 minutes to speak during Committee of Supply debates while elected opposition MPs and Government Parliamentary Committee chairpersons have 20 minutes each. PAP backbenchers have 18 minutes as well, unless they are the mover of a cut under a Head of Expenditure, where they will get an additional two minutes.
3.	Resources	Unlike elected MPs, NCMPs and NMPs are not allocated a budget for legislative assistant (LA) and special assistant (SA). The current budget is S$1,300 per month for LA and S$500 per

Table 1:   (*Continued*)

SN	Area	Specifics
		month for SA. Prior to J. B. Jeyaretnam becoming an NCMP, NCMPs had such support but that was taken away in 1997, four days before the then parliamentary term started. That prompted a debate in Parliament between Jeyaretnam and then Leader of the House Wong Kan Seng over the abrupt cancellation of the support.[4] Wong said it was "absurd" that Jeyaretnam implied that he represented the voters of Cheng San Group Representation Constituency (GRC) and that he was making "hypothetical claims to take responsibility for 45,000 voters", which would be the job of the elected MP. With the change to the NCMP scheme in 2017, this support is still unavailable to NCMPs. This issue of the lack of legislative support was raised by NCMP Leong Mun Wai in Parliament in May 2023.[5] Leader of the House Indranee Rajah reiterated the same argument used by Wong in 1997 that this support is not available for NCMPs and NMPs as they have lesser workload and no duties to constituents.
4.	Allowance	NCMPs receive 15% of the allowance of MPs. Based on the frequently asked questions section of the Public Service Division website, this works out to be S$28,900 per annum (S$2,408) per month.[6] The government turned down a recommendation by a government-appointed committee in 2017 to adjust the allowance to 20% to coincide with the granting of NCMPs with full voting rights.[7]

NCMPs' limited voting rights: How much does it matter?
Reflections by Yee Jenn Jong, former NCMP (2011–15)
The inability to vote on certain matters did not bother me during my time in Parliament. As NCMP, I spoke at great lengths on many occasions in areas which were also outside of the voting rights of

NCMPs. If the speeches contain important points, the press and the social media would pick them up and report, which is an important point in influencing policymaking.

All parliamentarians, NCMPs and NMPs included, can raise questions to ensure clarity in the government's intent on particular aspects in the phrasing of the law. Statements made by Ministers in Parliament clarifying aspects of a bill can be referenced in our Singapore courts to support in the interpretation of the law.

The ability to vote would also not make any difference to change any outcome. The maximum number of NCMPs is currently set at 12, which will be the case when there is not a single opposition MP elected. In a parliament with 93 elected MPs and nine NMPs, even if all the opposition MPs and NCMPs and even the NMPs voted against the PAP, it would still be below 33%. If the PAP does not lift the party's whip, all bills and all amendments to the Constitution will easily pass.

Given the vast imbalance in numbers between the opposition and the PAP, on the occasions when there were opposing votes, the dissent is recorded by those opposing saying "No" and those supporting saying "Aye". The Speaker would simply decide whether there had been more "Ayes" compared to "Noes". Sometimes, a division of parliament will be called to formally record the names of parliamentarians supporting, opposing or abstaining. Only in such circumstances would it technically matter if NCMPs had the right to vote as their names could be recorded. It would not change the outcome of the voting but will just increase the votes against.

Raising important issues, influencing policymaking

Reflections by Steve Chia, former NCMP (2001–06)

The NCMP scheme has a positive effect for NCMPs who actively speak up and raise issues in Parliament. It gives prominence to the loser candidates, who otherwise will be just like one of many other election losers — politicking in public, instead of being an effective politician. He/she now has a national platform to raise issues of national importance.

I believe that I did well during my term in the 10th Parliament. I raised the most questions in that term. The Home Affairs Minister Wong Kan Seng was forced to make changes to the house rules and to limit the number of questions an MP can ask to only three per seating.

I raised pertinent and important issues. Till today, many people still remembered Minister of State Cedric Foo's reply to me "that the purpose of 'white horse' labels in SAF is to ensure that they are not to be specially treated." Most people could not believe it.

I made the important argument that we need to take greater care of our pioneer generation of elders. They worked and earned Third World salaries to help propel Singapore into a First World environment. Now they are living in an expensive First World environment with the limited CPFs from their hard earned Third World income. We must and should do more to take care of the pioneer generations of people. Ten years later, the government took my arguments and came up with a Pioneer Generation package to help them.

I also argued for a greater distinction between citizens and permanent residents (PRs). During that time, PRs enjoyed almost all the same benefits, privileges and subsidies as a citizen, except for the right to vote. So I asked, "What are the benefits to bring a Singaporean?" That was also a reason why many Singaporeans have given up their citizenship in the past.

With that awakening, the PAP Government started re-working their policy differentiations making for a clearer and significant distinction between citizens and PRs. This has led to now more foreign people wanting to be citizens, and lesser citizens wanting to give up their Singapore citizenship anymore. Membership indeed has greater privileges now, and more foreigners are wanting to join our club.

And the people's realisation that a vocal responsible Opposition indeed brings more benefits to the people of Singapore. Many people are awakened to this important understanding and so subsequently they voted more favourably for the Opposition, especially for the more credible opposition candidates from credible parties.

Taking up NCMP seats while criticising the scheme: A contradiction?
Reflections by Leon Perera, former NCMP (2015–20) and former MP (2020–23)

Some have said that it is a contradiction for opposition parties to criticise the NCMP scheme and yet take up NCMP seats. However, taking up NCMP seats is akin to making the best of a bad situation. With its parliamentary supermajority, the ruling party controls the levers of power and can fine-tune the NCMP scheme and other electoral 'innovations' as it sees fit. Taking up NCMP seats enables opposition parties to gain valuable voices in Parliament to advocate for their ideas and to enable their leaders to gain experience. Given the extent of Singapore's unlevel political playing field and the odds stacked against them, opposition parties do not have the luxury of declining NCMP seats on grounds of principle.

Depending on the culture of the party and the character and inclinations of the individual NCMP, the work of an NCMP can be as demanding as that of a fully elected MP. Some NCMPs have been very active in walking the ground, sometimes in multiple constituencies. Some NCMPs have also served as non-elected town councillors.

NCMPs: No less an MP
Reflections by Leong Mun Wai, NCMP (since 2020)[8]

"At the end of the day, it is [about] ourselves. In Parliament, your mind and composure are very important. Because once you stand there and you think that you are a second-class MP, then you are out already. So of course, we hope the system will change in the future to truly formalise it, or that we have proportional representation so that we can be full-fledged MPs."

> ### *Reflections by Hazel Poa, NCMP (since 2020)*[9]
> "I do not feel any less [an MP] just because I am an NCMP. If we had a proportional representation system, our vote share of over 48% in West Coast GRC, versus the PAP under 52% — that margin was very tiny. And if we had the proportional representation system, we would have been full-fledged MPs. So to me, I don't see that we are any less an MP. I genuinely feel that we have earned the right to be in Parliament as well."

Undeniably, subtle differences in rights and support for NCMPs can make one feel that they had gotten into Parliament in an inferior position, at the 'generosity' of the PAP for enabling this scheme.

The differentiated treatment for NCMPs prior to April 2017 had not deterred them from making active contributions in Parliament. In the 2011–15 parliamentary term, Lianhe Zaobao did an analysis of the speech count of all parliamentarians at mid term in April 2014. NCMP Yee Jenn Jong was listed as having the highest speech count amongst male parliamentarians and joint highest overall. NCMP Gerald Giam and NCMP Lina Chiam were also listed amongst the top in their participation in Parliament.[10] In the 2015–20 term, NCMP Leon Perera and NCMP Dennis Tan were in the top three in speech count.[11]

The current NCMPs, Leong Mun Wai and Hazel Poa have also been very active in using all aspects of the parliamentary platform. They have filed four full motions in under three years — on the hot topics of foreign talent (including the India-Singapore Comprehensive Economic Cooperation Agreement or CECA) and public housing policies, as well as for an 'independent and impartial' Speaker of Parliament and the suspension of then Minister S. Iswaran whilst investigations were ongoing on alleged corruption against him. These were extensively debated upon and have brought the issues up into the national agenda. Only two parliamentarians are required to file for a full motion and the NCMP platform has been quite useful for their party to put issues out for national debates.

There are also additional parliamentary appointments which have seen opposition MPs, including NCMPs, as well as NMPs being placed onto select committees. NCMP Leong Mun Wai is a member of the Public Petitions Committee. Other opposition MPs and NMPs are or have been members of various select committees of Parliament. WP MPs Louis Chua and Jamus Lim are currently in the Public Accounts Committee and Estimate Committee, respectively while Leon Perera sat in the Public Accounts Committee as NCMP from 2016–20, and in the NMP Selection Committee as an MP from 2020–23. These are but a few examples.

Parliament sometimes would select opposition MPs, including NCMPs, as well as NMPs for overseas trips requiring representation by parliamentarians. In such matters, the involvement of NCMPs seem to be on par with that of elected MPs.

Differences with NMPs

Up till 2017, there were no differences in the allowances, support level and rights of NMPs compared to NCMPs. With the changes in 2017, NCMPs can now vote on all matters in Parliament while NMPs still cannot vote on constitutional amendments, motions to remove the President, motions of no-confidence in the Government, and supply and money Bills.

The most important difference is in their entry into Parliament. NMPs are intended to be non-partisan and hence cannot be a member of any political party when serving. Most were never members of political parties though some were previously members of the PAP and had stepped down before their appointment as NMPs such as Calvin Cheng and Tan Su Shan.[12] After the initial batch of NMPs, NMPs are now intended to represent the interest of functional groups, though there has been constant debate over the years whether it is beneficial to tie NMPs to functional groups.

When the NMP scheme was proposed in 1988, Dr Tan Cheng Bock, who was then a PAP MP, voted against it despite the party's whip not being lifted. Tan felt strongly that it was an issue of responsibility — NMPs have no constituents to hold them accountable.

In a podcast in 2020, Dr Tan continued to speak on why he was against the NMP scheme.[13]

"When you go to Parliament to speak, you speak with conviction, representing a sector of the population who voted for you… If you don't have that responsibility… you've got no mandate…". Tan also felt that without the need to contest in an election, they "would never understand the needs of the electorate."

Tan was concerned that NMPs would only speak on their pet topics — "They will go to the House and talk about their hobby-horse subjects. Not about the problems (relating to) HDB flats, or the current climate of problems in Singapore… There are other people who only talk about arts. This is not right. An MP, when you go into the House, must be able to talk about a wide range of subjects. They should not be given the opportunity to use Parliament to speak on their hobby-horse subject."

Are NCMPs 'Duckweeds'? The Roles of the NCMP ◆

Despite his continued reservations, Dr Tan admitted that there have been NMPs in the past who have deserved credit, such as Professor Walter Woon, who pushed a Private Member's Bill that later became the Maintenance of Parents Act.

Functioning as a team: WP's MPs and NCMPs
Reflections by Yee Jenn Jong, former NCMP (2011–15)

NCMPs enter Parliament through General Elections, though as losing candidates. They are therefore tied closely to party politics. In my time as NCMP, then WP leader Low Thia Khiang made no differentiation between the duties of MPs and NCMPs in Parliament. We functioned as a team on all matters. Each parliamentarian was given two to three government ministries to shadow and to further help as co-lead in at least another two ministries. I was to track bills and issues for the Ministry of Education, Ministry of Trade and Industry and Ministry of Finance. I was also to assist in the Ministry of Health and Ministry of Social and Family. We were also free to raise issues related to any other ministries. In my term in Parliament, I had spoken on issues across all ministries.

When we had to tackle large and contentious issues, we functioned as a team, agreeing first on our position, then on the order of speech and points to be raised by each, and who would conclude the debate.

This would be vastly different from how NMPs function in Parliament as they are meant to be unaffiliated with any

71

political party. They do however represent specific function groups such as environment, labour, businesses, sports, the arts, and so on.

During my time in Parliament as had also been in the past, some NMPs had voted against the PAP such as NMPs Faizah Jamal, Laurence Lien and Janice Koh in the debate on the Population White Paper and on the Public Order (Additional Temporary Measures) Bill sparked by the Little India riot of 2013. Hence, while they are without party affiliation, NMP do sometimes vote against proposals by the PAP as they are individually convicted.

Comparison with other political systems

Proportional representation

Singapore selects representatives for Parliament based on the Westminster system of first-past-the-post (FPTP). The candidate with the most votes in a constituency wins the right to represent that constituency in Parliament. There are other parliamentary systems which allow non-winners to be represented in Parliament. The most common is based on proportional representation (PR), which a number of territories subscribed to. There are also Mixed Member Proportional Representation systems such as in Taiwan and New Zealand — some MPs are elected from constituencies, while others are picked from party lists, based on the proportion of the total votes each party gets.

During the 2016 parliamentary debate on changes to the NCMP scheme, PM Lee Hsien Loong rejected the PR system, citing that "It would result in political parties based on race or religion. It would encourage political leaders to champion the demands of their particular segment, against the broader interests of Singapore. It would divide us, rather than bring us together."[14]

Singapore's NCMP scheme is adjusted from its FPTP system. In FPTP, the linkage between constituents and the MP is stronger than in a PR system where multiple MPs are selected from a much larger district. Furthermore, there is already an elected constituency MP officially recognised by government agencies to serve residents in the district that also has elected the NCMP. Hence in Singapore, the NCMP is strongly disadvantaged compared to constituency MPs, particularly in trying to seek re-election.

The NCMP scheme is a system that has no comparison in other democratic countries. It is a uniquely Singapore's way of preserving the ruling party's dominance in Parliament amid the electorate's growing desire of seeking an alternative voice as evidenced from poll results. When the scheme was conceived, around 30% support for the opposition only resulted in just one or two elected seats out of some 80 seats. With around 40% supporting the opposition in the 2011 and 2020 general elections, it resulted in around 10% elected opposition representation in Parliament.

Mauritius' best losers system

Perhaps the closest to the NCMP scheme is in Mauritius.[15,16] It has a 'best losers system' (BLS) to ensure fair representation of its ethnic minorities. Emeritus Senior Minister Goh Chok Tong had referred to Mauritius' system as an inspiration for Singapore's NCMP scheme.

Mauritius' National Assembly — its Parliament — consists of 70 members, 62 directly elected for five-year terms in multi-member constituencies and eight additional members, known as 'best losers', appointed by the Electoral Supervisory Commission to ensure that ethnic and religious minorities are equitably represented.

After a general election, the Electoral Supervisory Commission may nominate up to a maximum of eight additional members with a view to correct any imbalance in community representation in Parliament.

BLS is essentially a tool for fair representation in Parliament across four categories of people group: Hindu, Muslim, General Population and Sino-Mauritian. There is a mathematical way to compute representation through the 62 elected members and to balance out by having best losers from under-represented people groups.

We can view this system as an international example of inclusive political systems which Singapore tries to have through having a designated minority race in a GRC. BLS is not designed to achieve multi-party political representation which Singapore has tried to have via the NCMP scheme.

The reference to NCMPs as duckweeds

The very name, Non-Constituency Member of Parliament, already made it very clear that the Member does not represent any constituency. There is already an elected MP in the very constituency the NCMP had stood in. The role of MP is to look after constituents in that constituency. The NCMP is neither given access to any community facilities to organise activities or hold meet-the-people sessions in his or her capacity as a parliamentarian, nor recognition by government agencies as an official representative for the constituents.

Serious limitations for NCMPs

"Sir, in addition there are serious limitations to NCMP seats and it is important to highlight to Singaporeans these limitations. Besides not being able to vote on critical matters, we are considered as lacking in official capacity to represent the people. This was brought home in 1997 when Mr J. B. Jeyaretnam, who was then NCMP, filed a parliamentary question asking whether any directive had been given to Government departments not to reply to letters sent by him as NCMP. In the exchange which followed, the Home Affairs Minister reiterated the fact that NCMPs do not represent any particular constituency and, therefore, the Government departments would only respond to letters by elected MPs or grassroots advisers on behalf of residents in those areas.

"I have my own experiences of this reality. I have been doing house visits in Aljunied GRC for several years. The residents have raised certain concerns to me which I have highlighted in Parliament as issues, where appropriate. However, I have no official capacity to write letters on their behalf regarding their specific cases, though I would very much want to."

— Sylvia Lim, then an NCMP, during the debate on the Parliamentary Elections (Amendment) Bill, 27 April 2010

No difference in Parliament, major differences on the ground

Reflections by Yee Jenn Jong, former NCMP (2011–15)

While I felt no real difference in my role or inferiority in my contribution in Parliament as NCMP, there was a huge difference when it comes to ground activities compared to that of elected opposition MPs.

As an NCMP, my goal was to contest again in future elections with the aim to receive the mandate of the electorate. That proved very difficult with the Joo Chiat SMC that I had contested and lost narrowly in at GE2011. We did not have access to any community facilities. We continued weekly house visits to residents. I also assisted in meet-the-people sessions in areas won by WP. These enabled me to keep in touch with issues on the ground to raise them in Parliament.

About seven weeks before GE2015, the Electoral Boundaries Review Committee (EBRC) announced that Joo Chiat SMC was absorbed in Marine Parade GRC, forcing me to move to a five-man GRC to contest. Compared to elected MPs who had access to facilities for grassroots work, conduct meet-the-people sessions and represent the constituents to government agencies and had town council responsibilities, the NCMP has far fewer opportunities to develop roots. The EBRC has taken out SMCs that did better for the opposition and merged these into nearby GRCs at the next GE.[17]

I agree with Low's use of the duckweed analogy to describe the NCMP position given my frustrations trying to anchor myself to the Joo Chiat SMC. Nevertheless, the NCMP position was useful as it provided me with a national platform and opportunities to make an impact in Parliament. With the lack of ground presence, I felt more driven to make my impact through active participation in Parliament.

Rare to find NCMPs becoming MPs in same constituency contested

Reflections by Leon Perera, former NCMP (2015–20) and former MP (2020–23)

NCMPs lack the ability to engage constituents through the operations of the Town Council (TC) in the ward they contested in. The TC can be a way to add value to the lives of residents and also to demonstrate competence in municipal management. In this sense, NCMPs are indeed handicapped.

It is important to note that there are hardly any examples of any NCMP who went on to become fully elected MPs *in the constituency they contested in to become NCMPs* (Sylvia Lim being the only exception). The narrative that a successful NCMP would have a good chance of winning the next election in the same ward he/she lost earlier is not borne out by the facts. This underlines the limitations built into the NCMP role but also probably reflects the overall unlevel playing field that opposition parties face, which makes winning elections so difficult for them.

"Congratulations duckweed Goh!"

Facebook post by Daniel Goh, former NCMP (2016–20), January 2016

I was first notified of the NCMP motion passing when a good friend texted me, while I was washing dishes after dinner, "congratulations duckweed Goh!" I had a good laugh, though this is serious business through and through. (some comments deleted for brevity)

Mr Low is right: NCMPs are essentially duckweeds. He is using a Chinese flower metaphor in a very natural way, the significance and nuances of which many of us, Anglophones, don't understand. Very crudely, it means NCMPs are like pretty flowers that sink no roots, floating about and contradicting the values of harmony and community. Objectively, this is true in the long run, and I am with the WP MPs and the party opposing the NCMP scheme. But for me, personally, at this point in my life, and as I see it, at this point in Singapore's history, the principle of national service trumps the political principle of opposing the NCMP scheme. If my country sees fit that I contribute as duckweed, then it is my honour to be duckweed Goh. It is no insult; it is a privilege.

In any case, as a good man emailed me to tell me, for Anglophones such as us, duckweeds are not altogether negative, as they are seen as resilient and prolific plants valued as livestock feed, for water purification and for alternative biofuel. That is, to feed, to clarify and to drive the greater good in our shared commons. And so I hope and will strive, wish me Godspeed.

Less interactions with voters
Reflections by Hazel Poa, NCMP (since 2020)[18]

"The lack of a constituency has a big impact on us [as NCMPs], in that there is less interaction with voters. We also face constraints in securing venues to hold activities. It limits our interactions for getting feedback from residents. And that will impact on the kind of issues that we can bring into Parliament."

Lack of a constituency base
Reflections by Steve Chia, former NCMP (2001–05)

"The main challenge is basically the lack of a constituency base. Without a base to operate and expand from, there is limited groundwork I could do. So the limitations became a focused opportunity for me to make sure that I speak, raise a lot of important pertinent points and do well in Parliament."

MPs and NCMPs: Like day and night
Gerald Giam, former NCMP (2011–15) and MP (since 2020), in an interview with Channel NewsAsia in 2021[19]

"The adjustment (between being MP and NCMP) is almost like night and day because when you are an elected MP, people expect you to solve their problems...

"To me, being an opposition MP allows me a bit more freedom to be able to hear the feedback from the ground, I think people are quite open (to) sharing with me what their real concerns with the government policies are."

Looking at the consistent active participation of all NCMPs since the start of the scheme, NCMPs did not seem inhibited by the lack of certain voting rights or support level. To this end, the NCMP scheme did fulfil the PAP's objective of having active alternative voices in Parliament, including to engage with Ministers and PAP backbenchers.

The duckweed issue pertains more to the inability of NCMPs to develop political muscles to root themselves to a constituency to provide a better pathway back to Parliament for subsequent terms. As observed by Perera in the above interview, only Lim managed to be elected in the same constituency she had contested in as NCMP, and that too was in the extraordinary circumstances of the general election in 2011, especially with Low vacating the Hougang seat. That in essence, reflects the opposition's general objection with this scheme as it can hinder the development of a truly functioning multi-party political system.

6

Views from Political Observers

Loke Hoe Yeong & Yee Jenn Jong

After 40 years of the Non-Constituency Member of Parliament (NCMP) scheme, should Singapore retain it? Should the scheme be further refined? In this chapter, we speak political observers for their views. If they had the chance to revamp the political structures in Singapore including the NCMP scheme, what would it look like?

NCMP scheme has not deterred votes for the opposition

"I think there is value in keeping the scheme, since it has been shown to not have deterred voters from choosing the opposition. The reality is we operate in a dominant one-party system. Any assessment of whether an electoral innovation is necessary must be done in light of this political context. Given the People's Action

Party (PAP) dominance, and my assessment that since the NCMP does not deter voting for the opposition, it should stay.

"When or if we have a Parliament without a PAP supermajority, then maybe, we can discuss removing it."

— Assistant Professor Walid Jumblatt Bin Abdullah, School of Social Sciences, Nanyang Technological University

NCMP scheme could be democracy-enhancing

"Keep the scheme for sure. At the least, the mechanism helps to provide for a minimum level of opposition voices in Parliament. This is important because our electoral rules — first past the post in single-member districts and multi-member districts — frequently produces extreme supermajorities (around 95% of seats for the PAP) despite lower levels of vote share (70% or below). This means that around 25% or more of the population who do not vote for the PAP are unrepresented. One could argue that NCMPs provide for the representation of this unrepresented population.

"Furthermore, in terms of its impact on opposition parties, the NCMP scheme helps opposition members gain familiarity with Parliament as an institutional arena — its rules, its dos and don'ts, and its limits. We can already see such learning with the Progress Singapore Party (PSP). In addition, it helps provide a legitimate ground for the opposition to promote its policy agenda and to sharpen its differentiation with the PAP. Come election time, we can surmise that voters benefit from clearer agenda differentiation in between the various political parties.

"For these reasons, the NCMP scheme can be said to be democracy-enhancing in a fuller sense of the term 'democracy', even though most critics argue otherwise (with their focus on who wins or loses in each electoral district only)."

NCMPs: Their numbers and allowance

"Actually, I would suggest that maybe the NCMP scheme could be enhanced. I would increase the NCMP/NMP (Nominated Member of Parliament) allowance from the current annual S$28,900.[1] This works out to just over S$2,400 per month, which is far too little for their time and efforts, and to hire research assistants. I would note that S$2,400 per month is less than the reported median starting salary for polytechnic fresh graduates (S$2,550 per month) and polytechnic post-National Service graduates (S$2,800 per month) as reported in the 2022 graduate employment survey.

"Furthermore, I would suggest that the minimum number of opposition MPs be fixed at a proportion of the total number of elected parliamentarians, rather than an arbitrary number of 9 or 12. Say, hypothetically for example, 20% of elected parliamentarians. So following this example, if there are 93 parliamentarians to be elected (as in the 2020 General Election), then the minimum number of opposition MPs should be approximately 18 (rounded down). If 18 or more opposition parliamentarians are elected, then there will be no NCMPs. But if less than 18 opposition parliamentarians are elected, then they will be topped up to 18 by the NCMP scheme.

"If we care about bringing diverse voices into Singapore's Parliament as a law-making, policy-debating, and executive-scrutiny institution, I think schemes like NCMP and NMP are useful but artificial constructs with no other parallel anywhere in the world.

"We really got to think more about proportional representation (PR) as an electoral rule, rather than have first-past-the-post electoral system only. For many voters in many territories in the world, like Germany, New Zealand, Thailand, Taiwan, and Japan, they have both a vote to vote for their constituency MP and a PR vote for the political party. This creates more legitimacy and better focus on political parties as channelling diverse interests, rather than artificial constructs like "opposition", "arts community", or "business community".

— Assistant Professor Elvin Ong, Department of Political Science, National University of Singapore

Time to dump it

"I was never comfortable with the NCMP scheme. The official intention was to have a plurality of voices in Parliament. I never bought that argument. I believed it was a sneaky way of telling Singaporeans: Vote for PAP but you can still get opposition voices in Parliament. Maybe the PAP didn't realise it, it gave those who came in through the backdoor a chance to show their worth and become full MPs. Sylvia Lim is one example.

"And I don't believe that voters go to the ballot box with the NCMP scheme in mind. The time has come to dump this quirk in our electoral system."

— PN Balji, former editor of *The New Paper* and *TODAY*, and author of *Transition: The Story of PN Balji* and *Reluctant Editor: The Singapore Media as Seen Through the Eyes of a Veteran Newspaper Journalist*

A sunset clause for the NCMP scheme

Written interview with Associate Professor Eugene Tan, former NMP (2012–14), December 2023

1. Should Singapore keep the NCMP scheme or abolish it? Why?

As I see it, the NCMP scheme will become redundant when the number of elected opposition MPs hits a critical mass (say, a quarter of elected MPs). But until we get there, there is every value in retaining the scheme.

This ensures, in the words of Article 39(1)(b) of the Singapore Constitution, "the representation in Parliament of a minimum number of Members from a political party or parties not forming the Government". It promotes, albeit imperfectly, some degree of representativeness of Parliament.

Singapore voters have shown that they do not shun voting the opposition merely because of the NCMP scheme. They do know the difference between an elected opposition MP and an NCMP. Opposition political parties should acknowledge this rather than insist that the NCMP scheme undermines their electoral prospects.

Until Singapore voters regularly elect about a quarter of all MPs from the opposition, the NCMP scheme — on balance — benefits the opposition parties. That is why no political party has declined the NCMP seats since the 1988 General Election.[2] It has particularly proven to be most advantageous to the Workers' Party (WP) which has seen four of their NCMPs become elected MPs. The NCMP scheme has been a profitable springboard for the WP.

I would say that Singapore politics is the poorer without the NCMP scheme. True, the NCMP scheme is and must be seen as a stop-gap measure. While it is often said that the scheme is meant to benefit the ruling PAP, the parliamentary discourse would be the poorer without the NCMP scheme. So even if both the opposition and the PAP benefit from the scheme, the ultimate victor is Singapore and Singaporeans.

2. Why do you think the PAP increased the number of NCMPs in GE2011 and GE2020? Was it a coincidence that the opposition subsequently made gains as the NCMP numbers increased? Did the increase benefit the opposition or the PAP — or neither?

The more the NCMP seats, the better it is for the opposition in having their candidates who narrowly lost to the PAP to become "declared elected" NCMPs. Instead of seeing it as a "consolation prize", it is what the NCMP makes of his or her time in Parliament.

Singaporeans do not accord less weight to what an NCMP says in Parliament merely because he/she is an NCMP.

The increase in the number of NCMP seats for the 2011 and 2020 general elections did not result in fewer elected seats for the opposition; in both cases, the WP gained more elected seats. For me, this is a data point that the NCMP seats do not deter voters from voting for the opposition.

Similarly, while causality is hard to prove, I would still argue that the WP's NCMPs used their time fruitfully and their NCMP stints as the staging ground for their successful electoral campaigns in 2011 (Sylvia Lim) and 2020 (Gerald Giam, Dennis Tan and Leon Perera).

3. **As the political landscape in Singapore evolves, various proposals to adjust or improve the NCMP scheme have been put forward. If given the chance to relook and revamp the scheme, how would you reimagine it? Why?**

I don't think NCMPs should be permitted to vote on constitutional amendments. Given the gravity of constitutional amendments, this should be reserved only for elected MPs.

While an NCMP is unlikely to make any difference to the voting outcome on such amendments, I see the move in 2016 as one of trying to uplift the status of the NCMP but in so doing compromises the sanctity of the Constitution.

Secondly, I would also raise the minimum requirement for a candidate to have polled to 33% (from the current threshold of 15%) of the total number of votes (other than rejected votes) polled at the election in the electoral division contested by him or her as a prerequisite to be an NCMP. While all NCMPs since 1988 had polled way above 33%, I think the scheme would be better received and respected if the minimum proportion of votes required is pitched at a more competitive level. At 15%, that is only slightly higher than what it takes for an election candidate not to lose the election deposit.

I would also inscribe into the Constitution a "sunset clause" that Parliament would not have NCMPs when the number of elected opposition MPs is at least one-third the total number of elected seats. Again, practically, this does not change the ability of the Opposition to alter parliamentary dynamics such as constitutional amendments. Rather, what it signals is that the NCMP scheme is but a stop-gap measure in light of the one-party dominance in Singapore.

In addition, the law that governs the filling of a vacated NCMP seat should be relooked. Currently, the law provides that Parliament may, immediately after a general election, fill a vacated NCMP seat (that is, an "NCMP-elect" declining to accept the NCMP seat). This should be changed to make the one-time filling of such a vacated seat automatic, without Parliament having to decide whether to fill the seat or not.

Next, the law should prohibit any "intra-party" transfer of an NCMP seat. After the 2015 General Election, the WP picked up three NCMP seats: one from Punggol East SMC (48.23% for Ms Lee Li Lian), one from Fengshan SMC (42.5% for Mr Dennis Tan) and one from East Coast GRC (39.27%). WP had decided that from their East Coast GRC team, Mr Leon Perera would take up the NCMP seat, together with Mr Tan. However, Ms Lee did not take up her seat. For what appeared to be strategic considerations, the WP decided that Assoc Prof Daniel Goh, another candidate from the WP's East Coast GRC team, would take the place of Ms Lee.

The WP effectively transferred the NCMP seat meant for Ms Lee to A/P Goh. Should such an intra-party transfer of NCMP seats be prohibited, a vacated NCMP seat cannot be taken up by another losing election candidate from the same party but who had contested in a different constituency.

The overall intent of the last two proposals is to ensure the integrity of the NCMP scheme. Automatically filling a vacated NCMP seat avoids a situation where the filling of a vacated NCMP seat is at the will of the ruling party. Prohibiting an intra-party transfer of NCMP seats prevents a situation where an opposition party can act anti-democratically by thwarting the expressed political choice of the electorate.

There is a tendency to overlook the democratic element that underpins the NCMP scheme. The Parliamentary Elections Act 1954 provides that the NCMP seats are to be filled on the basis of the percentage of the votes polled in a general election (the so-called "best losers" requirement). Clearly, the voters' preference is determinative with regards to the filling of NCMP seats. As such, opposition parties should not be allowed to go against the choice of voters in filling NCMP seats because that is tantamount to letting a party, rather than the voters, decide on the NCMPs.

It should also be noted that the WP has opposed the NCMP scheme from its inception and that it would abolish the scheme if it were the Government. The WP's premise is that elections should not dilute the individual voter's voice and should therefore only be run on single member seats, with individual MPs fully accountable to constituents. However, in reality, the WP adopts a different reasoning when it says that it would allow an eligible WP candidate to take up a NCMP seat so as to contribute to parliamentary debates and because "the struggle for a functional democracy… must be fought from within the existing system".

4. **Would you like to share other comments on the NCMP scheme or on Singapore's current political landscape?**

Like its Nominated MP (NMP) counterpart, the NCMP scheme will eventually become irrelevant — it's not a question of whether but rather when.

It will become irrelevant when we have either a two-party parliamentary democracy or a multiparty parliamentary democracy.

But until that comes to pass, NCMPs still have a key role to play in contributing to our parliamentary system of government and underscoring that a system of checks and balances, when properly utilised, can add to our system of government and governance.

In discussing the NCMP scheme, it is important to recognise it as part of the constitutional engineering that took place between 1984 and 1991. During this period, the NCMP scheme in 1984 kicked off the quartet of bold and controversial initiatives to create an autochthonous legislative system while keeping the trappings of the Westminster parliamentary model. The Group Representation Constituency (GRC) was introduced in 1988, the NMP scheme in 1990, and the elected presidency in 1991. This wave of institutional design coincided with the first leadership transition in independent Singapore.

But why?

The political intent of maintaining Parliament's relevance in a one-party dominant system necessitated innovations to promote and protect the central idea of representation. The PAP government recognised the need to ensure a minimum, if not nominal, representation of opposition and non-partisan parliamentarians. The pre-emptive nature of these constitutional innovations — the NCMP, GRC, NMP, Elected Presidency schemes — was evident even as the notion of representation was subtly relied upon to add legitimacy.

However, such moves should not be mistaken as an endeavour to deepen democratic tendencies. The NCMP scheme sought to keep pace with and manage the desire for more non-government voices in the legislature. This attempt to introduce non-PAP MPs was to ensure that Parliament would not be perceived as a *de facto* PAP party caucus, which could have the deleterious effect of not enabling Parliament to be the central platform for the debate on key matters of the day that affect Singapore and Singaporeans. In turn, this can help reduce the perception that Parliament, as the legislative body, was but a mere rubber stamp of law-making, budgetary and policy initiatives of the dominant Executive (the Cabinet). In other words, the one-party dominant system need not mean the enervation of checks and balances.

7

Views from the
Opposition

Loke Hoe Yeong & Yee Jenn Jong

The positions of opposition parties

The Workers' Party

When the scheme was first introduced in Parliament in 1984, J. B. Jeyaretnam was the only parliamentarian of the Workers' Party (WP) and indeed the only opposition MP. He voted to oppose the scheme and stated that his party would not accept any offers of a Non-Constituent Member of Parliament (NCMP) seat. At the ensuing general election, the party indeed rejected the seat offered to M.P.D. Nair.

The party however, subsequently accepted the seat when offered to Lee Siew Choh in 1988, and Jeyaretnam himself took up the position in 1997. Thereafter, all NCMP seats offered to the WP were accepted, these being to Sylvia Lim (2006), Gerald Giam (2011), Yee Jenn Jong (2011), Dennis Tan (2015), Leon Perera (2015), and Daniel Goh (2016), who took up the position after it was rejected by Lee Li Lian.

The public position of the party has been that the scheme can be abolished when there is a wider revamp to correct unfair electoral practices. In its latest manifesto released during the 2020 General Election, the party states, "The GRC system should be abolished and be replaced by Single Member Constituencies. Singaporeans have matured as a society to the point and there is now no evidence that Singaporeans vote solely along racial lines. Continuing the GRC system may, in fact, reinforce that which it seeks to counter, as the existence of GRCs may be taken to signal that ethnic minority candidates are unelectable on their own. With the abolition of GRCs and the removal of the Elections Department from the purview of the Prime Minister, the NCMP scheme can be discontinued as it would be unnecessary."

This position has been consistent in all recent manifestos since at least the 2006 General Election. Through various speeches in public and in Parliament, the party's acceptance of the NCMP positions despite its objection can be summarised as making the best out of a lopsided and uneven political playing field. This is akin to it rejecting the GRC scheme but still contesting in GRCs because it is an integral part of

> "The Workers' Party is a rational and responsible political party. We understand the political reality. We understand that the struggle for a functional democracy by a loyal Opposition must be fought from within the existing system under the law legislated by Parliament even though we disagree with that. Therefore, we do not oppose individual Members who are willing to sacrifice their time and energy to contribute to the national debate in Parliament."
>
> — Low Thia Khiang, former Secretary-General of the Workers' Party, in a speech to open the debate on the NCMP Motion on 29 January 2016

Singapore's political system. It is also for individual members offered the NCMP position to decide with the party's Central Executive Committee (CEC) of the day.

The Progress Singapore Party

The Progress Singapore Party (PSP) has no official position on the NCMP scheme in its manifesto for the 2020 General Election. The manifesto called for stronger alternative voices in Parliament and drew attention to the dominance of the People's Action Party (PAP) in Parliament (about 90%). Dr Tan Cheng Bock had outrightly rejected the post for himself prior to the general election in 2020. The party was offered two NCMP seats, which were taken up by Leong Mun Wai and Hazel Poa. Leong and Poa (see interview below) shared that it was up to the team being offered the positions to decide. The team met and agreed that the two would take up the positions.

The Singapore Democratic Party

The Singapore Democratic Party's (SDP) position appears similar to that of the WP — rejection of the scheme as a poor form of democracy but would be open to taking up the position as it is part of the existing political system.

"[The NCMP scheme] should be abolished as it is non-democratic, a distraction and undermines the elected parliamentary system. Having said that, it is here and we have to live with it. From my own field, it is like prescribing panadol for a patient with pneumonia or sepsis or some other severe bacterial infection.

We all know that the patient needs antibiotics but if the healthcare provider is not willing to allow appropriate antibiotics to be administered, then we just give the patient panadol on the grounds that perhaps it is better than nothing. Also at least if the patient dies, he or she will be a little less uncomfortable with panadol for the fever. As a number of academic observers have pointed out, democracy is dying slowly in Singapore (or being snuffed out) and I guess some palliative care with measures such as the NCMP scheme is better than nothing."

— Dr Paul Tambyah, Chairman, Singapore Democratic Party, in an email interview on 24 November 2023

The Singapore People's Party

The Singapore People's Party's (SPP) most recent manifesto for the 2020 General Election was silent on the NCMP post.

When the SPP's founding secretary-general Chiam See Tong was an MP in 1984, then as secretary-general of the SDP, he had opposed the scheme. He opposed the constitutional amendments in 2010 to increase the number of NCMP positions, along with other constitutional amendments. Prior to voting in the 2011 General Election, Chiam also stated that he would decline the seat if offered. An NCMP post was offered to Lina Chiam who contested in the Potong Pasir seat vacated by Chiam in 2011. The position was taken up by the party. In an email interview (see below), its current secretary-general Steve Chia is supportive of retaining the scheme.

Views of individual politicians

We also asked individual politicians for their views — if they had the chance to revamp the political structures in Singapore including the NCMP scheme, what would it look like?

On proportional representation

"One option is to have some kind of proportional representation. That way the PAP will not be able to continue to get away with getting 89% of the seats in Parliament with only 61% of the votes. There are many different ways of ensuring that the wishes of the electorate are respected. We have many very talented scholars in the social sciences in Singapore who can analyse the different proportional representation systems which are in use in Asia (and perhaps even Europe) and perhaps offer voters a real informed choice about how they can have a say in how they are governed."

— Dr Paul Tambyah, Chairman, Singapore Democratic Party, in an email interview on 24 November 2023

NCMPs useful when there are insufficient opposition MPs

"The NCMP scheme was definitely useful when there were not enough opposition MPs in Parliament. It is still useful today. There should be at least one fifth of seats (about 20) in Parliament catered to the opposition, whether elected or as NCMP. My proposal is to remove the Nominated Member of Parliament scheme and expand the total seats available to elected and non-elected opposition MPs to one fifth (currently about 20 seats) in Parliament.

"It is important to have opposition MPs in Parliament. It keeps the PAP government in check, and forces greater accountability of policies, words and actions. It will demand greater efforts from elected MPs to work the grounds, meet the residents, help the people and most importantly, to be humble and people grounded.

"It is clear that the scheme was introduced by the PAP government with the intention of providing a form of opposition representation in Parliament, and ensuring that voters have confidence in the political system, even if they do not vote for the ruling party.

"I think the scheme works well to complement elected opposition MPs. Imagine the day if the Workers' Party loses both GRCs and Hougang SMC. Without the NCMP scheme, then there would be no opposition MP in Parliament again. This should never happen again, for the good of Singapore."

— Steve Chia, former NCMP (2001–06), current Secretary-General of the Singapore People's Party

Voting opposition, getting the best of both worlds

"It is possible to turn the NCMP argument on its head. Instead of NCMPs making it unnecessary to vote opposition, it can be argued that by voting opposition, the voters get the best of both worlds — an opposition voice in Parliament, while the losing PAP candidates continue to serve as grassroots advisers on the ground, stewarding the work of the local People's Association-linked organisations… and the most electable of the losing PAP candidates would probably be parachuted into a safe PAP constituency at the next election and thus enter Parliament anyway.

"Voters should ask themselves this — if they want opposition voices in Parliament to nudge the PAP to change policies that they would like to see changed, would 12 NCMPs make the same impact as 12 fully elected opposition MPs? Surely not. Fully elected opposition MPs who won their electoral contests are more effective in nudging the PAP to implement policy changes. NCMPs would not have the same effect, as they lost their electoral races and thus do not possess the same mandate.

"Compared to NCMPs, Party leaders who are fully elected opposition MPs are better able to grow and develop their opposition parties to become successful organisations that can attract and retain talent and can develop and internalise the necessary know-how to run Town Councils. Victory in elections conduces talent attraction and organisation development. If Singapore is to develop viable, sustainable alternative parties to the PAP, those parties must seek more fully elected MP seats.

"It is important to note that there are hardly any examples of NCMPs who went on to become fully elected MPs in the constituency they contested in to become NCMPs (Sylvia Lim being the only exception). The narrative that a successful NCMP would have a good chance of winning the next election in the same ward he/she lost earlier is not borne out by the facts. This underlines the limitations built into the NCMP role but also probably reflects the overall unlevel playing field that opposition parties face, which makes winning elections so difficult for them.

"Sometimes the NCMP scheme is justified on the basis that it is a 'stabiliser' that reduces the risk of a freak election result where the PAP government loses power because voters picked opposition candidates to be an opposition and not the government. However, a quick look at the actual history of elections in Singapore shows that the likelihood of a freak election result that wipes out all fully elected opposition MPs is far, far higher than one where the PAP loses power. The PAP has not come even remotely close to losing power in an election since 1963. Fully elected opposition MPs were almost wiped out in the general elections in 2001 and 2015. Prior to this, Singapore had long stretches of time with no or hardly any fully elected opposition MPs. Most voters understand this.

"The scheme can be abolished. It tends to entrench the PAP's political dominance."

— Leon Perera, former NCMP (2015–20) and former MP (2020–23)

An interview with Leong Mun Wai and Hazel Poa

(This interview was conducted on 14 June 2023.)

KEY:
LMW — Leong Mun Wai
HP — Hazel Poa
YJJ — Yee Jenn Jong

NWM — Ng Wai Mun
LHY — Loke Hoe Yeong

NWM: Both of you are the current NCMPs. We want to get your thoughts on how it has been working as NCMPs, as well as the perspective you may have had before taking up the role.

YJJ: Opponents of the NCMP scheme believed that the PAP intended to use it to assure voters that there would always be an opposition presence in Parliament. This is to dissuade voters from voting in full opposition MPs. At every general election, the PAP will bring this up. Do you think that that has a useful effect on the mind of voters?

HP: For myself, initially, I was a bit worried that this would persuade voters not to vote in full opposition MPs, but the results of the 2020 General Election showed us very clearly that this has not been the case. The PAP improved the NCMP scheme after the 2015 General Election. They increased the number of NCMPs, and gave them the same voting rights as elected MPs.

Despite these changes, in the 2020 General Election, we saw more elected opposition MPs. I do not think that the scheme has had that effect of dissuading voters from voting in opposition MPs.

NWM: Do you think that conversation on NCMP, particularly during general elections, tends to dominate the campaign? Did it affect the issues that the opposition wanted to raise, but couldn't?

HP: When we do ground visits, hardly anybody ever raised that as an issue that they wanted to talk about. It is usually about bread-and-butter issues.

LMW: Like what Hazel said, the NCMP scheme was almost a non-issue in 2020. The government amended the terms of the NCMP in 2017. I think after 2015 General Election, in their optimistic mood, the PAP thought that it was time to kill off all the opposition. People were talking about whether they are going to have 100% control of the Parliament again.

During the press conference where I accepted the NCMP offer, I said "基本上，政府赔了夫人又折兵" (the government suffered a double loss). They amended the scheme to increase the number of NCMPs, but they did not benefit. In fact, they lost four more seats.

YJJ: Interestingly, looking at history, every time they increased the numbers of NCMPs, they actually lost more seats.

LHY: My sense is that the government increased the NCMP quota every time they sensed that would be more clamour for opposition voices, or that they felt that they were going to lose more seats. I wonder if you sense that that's been the case?

HP: That will be second guessing it.

NWM: I think most opposition parties, including the PSP, have come out to oppose the NCMP scheme, especially during election campaigns. And even as the PAP has made the position more substantive and more convincing for voters, they seem not to get the benefits of that. Does it change the PSP's position moving forward? Have you moderated your stance on the NCMP scheme? Or is the PSP still principally opposed to the NCMP scheme?

HP: At a party level, we have not really discussed this issue. But for me, personally, I have definitely shifted my position on the scheme. As I said, I was initially worried about the effect of the scheme on voters, but the 2020 General Election has shown that my fears were unfounded.

NWM: What is your stance on the scheme now?

HP: I think that it is a good scheme. It is a form of affirmative action. I do feel that the NCMP scheme is giving more opposition members an opportunity to be seen and heard — an opportunity that they would not have gotten if they had not been an NCMP. Personally, that is our experience. As to whether it is a boon or bane for us, that of course depends on an NCMP's own performance — whether they make good use of it or make a mess of it. It can go either way.

LMW: I think the NCMP scheme is a good step in the development of democracy in Singapore, although I must qualify that I don't think the PAP meant it that way. They had a different objective. But I think it is a positive step in the development of democracy nevertheless. That is why in recent years, many have likened the scheme to a proportional representation system. Worldwide, I think you cannot find many countries that only have a first-past-the-post system. Many countries have put in a mixture of proportional representation and first past the post. The exceptions are countries like Malaysia and the UK. Most European countries have proportional representation systems.

As democracy progresses, the demands of society and voters cannot be met by a first-past-the-post system alone. The first-past-the-post system has its pros and cons as well. We must continue to harness the pros, but minimise the cons. One way to minimise the cons is to have some level of proportional representation.

Of course, a proportional representation system also has its problems. Party leaders become very powerful because they determine the order in which candidates are ranked on the party list, which basically determines who gets to become an MP. In first past the post, party leaders can send candidates to difficult areas but they could still win if they campaign very hard. But if minority voices are not well organised in the first-past-the-post system, they will never stand a chance. So, when you have a proportional representation system, you would get the Green Party in Germany in, because they crossed the threshold of attaining 5% of the vote share at the 2021 Bundestag elections. If you represent a certain critical percentage of voters, then even if those votes are distributed around the whole country, a proportional representation system would recognise you as a political force while a first-past-the-post system would not.

And that, to me, reflects the demand of the voters. You cannot just allow a big party with good organisation to win it all. The small parties that come in and compete — if enough people support them, they should still get seats. All these issues are much talked about already. So, you can also regard the NCMP scheme as a variant of the proportional representation system. The purpose of proportional representation is to allow minority voices to be heard — that's the same with the NCMP scheme.

YJJ: Do you think then that the NCMP scheme is good enough to keep, or should we change it into a different mechanism? If you have proportional representation, you will not need NCMPs. The only country with something similar to the NCMP scheme is Mauritius. They do have a highest losing candidate scheme, but it is based on ethnicity. If a certain ethnic group is underrepresented, particularly the minority ethnic groups, then the representatives of those groups get in even if they have lost. That's the only other country with a NCMP-like scheme. Others use proportional representation to cater to minority voices. In your opinion, if we do away with the NCMP scheme, would you prefer a proportional representation system?

LMW: Yes, and have a certain threshold to cross. And use the proportional representation system to provide for minority representation. In a way, it's the same as in Mauritius, where you use the scheme to provide for the representation of minority voices. And in that scenario, what the PSP is thinking about is that Singapore should abolish the GRC scheme.

YJJ: Yes, that is another contentious point for the opposition — although the GRC scheme has now come back to haunt the PAP. Because, when they lose a GRC, it is also not easy for them to win it back. When some MPs in a team retire, the party can renew the slate with younger candidates.

LMW: Yes, although it has become difficult for the PAP to win a GRC back, it is not just because of the GRC scheme. It is the inherent strength of the first-past-the-post scheme that, in theory, benefits the incumbent. If you're there as an MP, you have a lot of resources to build up your base, provided that you are a hardworking MP.

NWM: Just to clarify, if we accept that the GRC system remains together with the NCMP scheme — since both of you seem to be of a positive view that there are certain benefits to having NCMPs…

LMW: … from the point of democratic development…

NWM: … Is the PSP, or you personally, in support of keeping the NCMP scheme in its current form? Or do you think it should evolve in a certain way?

LMW: We have not discussed this issue as a party yet so we will reserve our comments.

What we are saying is that we favour democratic development. So, if we take out the NCMP scheme, then you should put something else in its place.

NWM: I find it very interesting that you brought up the point about representing so-called minority voices, which is the spirit in which you are supporting the scheme. Singapore's NCMP scheme does not come with that minority requirement. Are there specific issues or voices from the public that you try to bring forth in Parliament that represent certain minority voices? Probably not only as regards ethnic minority representation, but from the opposition's perspective.

LMW: We did not set out to want to represent any minority group or views because we are a national party. We think that the role of an MP or NCMP is to bring up the views of all segments who may be facing difficulties or injustice. If there are some issues to bring up, we will bring them. In that sense we are also taking care of the minorities, but not for specific communities.

HP: So for example, like the debate on the Singapore-India Comprehensive Economic Cooperation Agreement. On the ground, we were getting feedback that people felt their jobs were being threatened by foreigners. This may not be the majority view. There are also other people who feel it is good to have foreign talent. But we had heard enough feedback to feel that it was important to bring up this issue. We have also spoken up on other issues as well, such as housing affordability and vaccination-differentiated measures.

YJJ: We want to talk about the effectiveness of using the NCMP platform to raise issues at the national level, and your personal experience with Parliament. What are the challenges and opportunities you faced as NCMPs? Do you experience some restrictions as an NCMP, even though they have now removed most of the restrictions? NCMPs still have two minutes less speaking time, right?

HP: Only the elected opposition MPs (and Government Parliamentary Committee Chairs) get 20 minutes. Apart from the speaking time, we are not given an allowance to engage legislative assistants. And of course, the biggest problem is that we have no constituency. The lack of a constituency has a big impact on us, in that we must actively create our own opportunities to interact with voters. We also face constraints in securing venues to hold activities. It limits our interactions for getting feedback from residents. And that will impact on the kind of issues that we can bring into Parliament.

YJJ: For venue permits, I do not think they will allow it for NCMPs. We are coming more into the topic of the duckweed analogy for NCMPs — that you cannot sink your roots into the ground at the constituency level. That will be a big disadvantage.

LMW: Yes, unless we have proportional representation.

NWM: Since they amended the NCMP scheme in 2017 to give NCMPs equal voting rights, have you seen that as a benefit? Is it something you can substantively exercise?

HP: I would say that under current circumstances, it really makes very little difference. Because the PAP has a supermajority. Whichever way we vote, it is not going to make any difference to the outcome. For now, I do not see it making any difference.

LMW: For the outcome, no, but in terms of the role of NCMP, it really enhances your self-esteem in that you can vote on important constitutional amendments in Parliament.

NWM: You have raised full motions as well. Could you elaborate on that?

LMW: For motions, there is no effect at all. NCMPs and MPs can raise motions. You just need at least two parliamentarians to call for one. If the MP who files a motion is the only one from their party, they will have to get some support from another party. And sometimes they may not lend such support. So, we are lucky that there are two of us from the same party.

YJJ: The NCMP scheme at least provides that parliamentary platform which allows PSP and yourselves to raise national issues, which has garnered public attention. Do you feel like there are some issues that you felt that have been very useful for yourselves and the party, especially in using this platform?

LMW: I think Parliament is a very special place. Any political party who aspires to be in play for the long term must understand Parliament. And even though we are NCMPs, we gain the same experience in Parliament as any other elected MP. The experience that we gain would benefit the PSP.

HP: And I will say that it is important for all issues, regardless of what it is. Not just certain issues. It is not the same to raise issues in Parliament and outside Parliament — the kind of exposure that you get, the kind of media attention that you get is totally different. In a way, if you raise something in Parliament, then the government will check if what you're saying is right or valid. Whereas if you say it outside, they will generally not bother. So, there's no validation. There may be greater legitimacy for a cause or issue when it is raised in Parliament.

NWM: I was wondering if you could give an example of a particular debate in Parliament where you feel there was a challenge, or there were limits as to what you can actually do to push your position?

LMW: You are going into an area faced not only by NCMPs. It is the situation faced by all opposition MPs, because there are such a small number of us. So only when that number greatly increases can we perhaps see the other side take us more seriously.

NWM: Do you think that having the role — having been in Parliament as an NCMP — does it help your political career? And did it help the party as a whole? What are the pros and cons for yourself and the party?

HP: That's a question the Workers' Party is better able to answer. There has been no election since we became NCMPs. It's difficult for us to assess that, whereas the Workers' Party has had years and years, and many elections, to comment from.

LMW: You can see from the growth of the Workers' Party that it is a major beneficiary of the NCMP scheme. But no NCMP from any other opposition party has managed to successfully retain their seat, either as an NCMP or an elected MP.

HP: For us, our visibility [as politicians] has definitely been raised. But as to the electoral effect, I think we are unable to tell yet.

NWM: There is also the increased visibility. For example, the confrontational stance and this is something that will sit in voters' mind, because you are so visible and you are debating in Parliament. Do you calibrate your debate style, taking into consideration that this is a visible role?

LMW: Of course, we learn on the job. Initially when you go into Parliament, you do not know what the rules are. Even if you read

Parliament's standing orders, you may not fully appreciate how Parliament operates.

So, you only can rely on experience. During the exchanges, you observe what ministers say, what the Speaker says, and how other people react, and how they react to what other people say. From there, you will know what the OB [out-of-bounds] markers are. So only when you know the OB markers can you then know what to say. As a result, I can now perform better because I now know where the OB markers are. In the beginning, I did not know. So, when the Ministers said something, I got worried that I might have broken certain rules and just stopped there. In hindsight I now realise I should not have stopped. Basically, experience is gathered over time. And of course, there are many things that prevent opposition MPs from making their thoughts known. There is a lot of trial and error. But this is not restricted to NCMPs. We all learn over time. And of course, as to certain labels being thrown at me, that is a matter of interpretation.

We are always conscious that we do not just hurt ourselves. Our party can be affected too. On the other hand, we do not need to be scared. As long as we speak based on facts, there should be no fear. And even if my presentation may not be the best sometimes, that's the real me. I have no fear about my presentation, because I'm very confident of my facts. I just stand up and lay down the facts. They may say it is a baseless allegation because they don't want to respond to me and that is their prerogative. I am not experienced enough yet to counter them, but I will be prepared to counter them at the next round. There were many instances where

I had laid out all the facts and they avoided a debate. And then they put labels on me. Of course, politics is a lot about optics. We have to be mindful of that. But I think if you ask me for advice for opposition MPs, don't be too concerned about this. Your role is to state the facts. Ask the questions. Do not worry too much about it, or that it may not go down well, or that you will be countered.

LHY: Speaking of labels, there is the unfortunate label that NCMPs are just the 'best losers'. Have you ever been made to feel that whenever you raise an issue in Parliament? Have your PAP counterparts perhaps reminded you that you are just the 'best loser', as they once reminded J.B. Jeyaretnam, and perhaps you don't have a mandate to speak on people's behalf?

HP: Actually, I am not bothered. To me, I do not feel any less just because I am an NCMP. Our vote share of over 48% in West Coast GRC, versus the PAP under 52% — that margin was very tiny. If we had a proportional representation system and the seats in a GRC were allocated based on vote share, we would have been returned as full-fledged MPs. So to me, I don't see that we are any less of an MP. I genuinely feel that we have earned the right to be in Parliament as well.

LMW: I take the same stance as Hazel, although sometimes in Parliament, there are some words or actions reflecting that. For example, some of the points that we raise will often be ignored, and the PAP will only focus on the Workers' Party in their reply. Maybe that was the way I felt. Nevertheless, in general, we do not really feel that we are just 'best losers'.

HP: To me, it's not important whether they show that kind of attitude or not. What's most important is what we ourselves think.

LMW: Correct. At the end of the day, it is ourselves. In Parliament, your mind and composure are very important. Because once you stand there and you think that you are a second-class MP, then you are out already. So of course, we hope the system will change in the future to truly formalise it, or that we have proportional representation so that we can be full-fledged MPs.

YJJ: Just a curious question about the party's decision, because there were some transitions. Earlier on, the party wanted both of you to focus more on Parliament and both of you resigned from the CEC. But now you are the Secretary-General and Vice-chairman. Would you say that the exposure and active participation in Parliament has helped you within the party to build a base for your political career?

LMW: Regarding that, Dr Tan Cheng Bock had convinced us to just concentrate on Parliament initially, because there was going to be a lot of work. And we do not have a legislative assistant. Everything is done by ourselves.

HP: It was not meant to be permanent. It was because we were so new and had very little support. And we did not have current MPs to guide us along.

NWM: Do you feel that the visibility you had as NCMPs helped gear towards that decision of the party to reappoint you back to the CEC?

LMW: We have never left the CEC. We have always been members of the CEC. It was the right timing for both of us to take on more roles in the party after gaining three years of experience in Parliament.

After three years, we know our roles in Parliament better. We do not need as much time to prepare Parliamentary Questions. Many things are a continuation of what we had raised earlier. We know the ropes and as a result, we are calmer. We can take on more responsibilities. It is actually a full-time job to be an MP.

YJJ: During the annual Budget debate, there are many parliamentary sittings. It is hard to take so many days of leave from work. I was fortunate to be running my own business when I was an NCMP.

LMW: Exactly. It is part of how things are made difficult for NCMPs. We are only provided with a very small allowance on the justification that we are not full MPs. So you have to juggle between your job and being an NCMP.

NWM: Has that been a very huge challenge for both of you over these past few years?

HP: For me, I also run my own business. So I have that flexibility to manage my own schedule. And as you know, you have to allocate a lot of time to the Budget debate every year. So far, it is still manageable, even though it is quite tough.

NWM: Another question is the decision to take up the NCMP role, especially after Dr Tan Cheng Bock and yourself mentioned that you would not take it up. What was the ensuing discussion that led to the eventual taking up? How do you weigh whether someone takes it up or not? And who do you put forward as a party to take up the NCMP?

LMW: First of all, the NCMPs must come from the GRC team.

HP: Dr Tan already said no, so it was just the four of us left. Among the group, we just talked. It was decided by the group.

NWM: You spoke about the institutional experience that you have, now that both of you have been learning the ropes. Have there been discussions on how to ensure that the institutional memory or experience benefits the party moving forward?

Also, this is the first time for the PSP to take up NCMP positions. What are some of the considerations on how you perform that role in Parliament, and has that helped the party to understand the parliamentary procedures better?

LMW: We have some occasional feedback sessions on why I raise certain things in Parliament, or for us to gather feedback on policies. We have these mechanisms within the party, and sometimes at the cadre level. Hazel and I now definitely have valuable institutional knowledge that we can pass down to others within the party, whether or not we are in Parliament in the future. As long as we have people in Parliament, we can give advice.

HP: We share what we can, but nothing compares to really experiencing it yourself. I feel that it is more effective when someone we are sharing our experience with is actually in Parliament. And when they are made to do the work, that is when the sharing will be more meaningful.

YJJ: If we still must live with the NCMP scheme, are there some things about the scheme you want to change?

LMW: I think there should be some formalisation of the status of NCMPs, not just as 'best losers'. So something in line with a proportional representation system will be recommended by me. As for working at the grassroots level, I do think that's something logical to ask for. Because every constituency has their own MP. So if there are MPs who get in through a proportional representation system, who don't have to work at the grassroots level, then it may not be fair to the constituency MPs. But as you asked me, I think MPs should be relieved of their municipal roles in the Town Councils. The MP should concentrate on policies at the national level.

So they should be advisers to Town Councils. Town Councils should be managed by the HDB.

YJJ: You will still be handicapped from contesting in West Coast GRC the next time round, because you will not have the ground exposure as the sitting MPs would have. You still cannot book any facilities to use for grassroots activities.

LMW: But if you have proportional representation, the party is almost always guaranteed some MPs. The rights to use facilities — that can be changed.

HP: I don't see that as an NCMP problem, I see that as a general problem. Why is it that the venues cannot be used for political purposes?

LMW: The elected MPs from the Workers' Party do not get access to the Citizens' Consultative Committees (CCC). And they are not made CCC advisers either...

HP: It is just not a level playing field.

8

Views from the People's Action Party
Is the NCMP Scheme Still Relevant?

With contributions from Goh Chok Tong and Inderjit Singh

How relevant is the Non-Constituency Member of Parliament (NCMP) scheme, 40 years on? In his own words, we hear from former Prime Minister — now Emeritus Senior Minister — Goh Chok Tong, a key architect of the NCMP scheme. We also posed this and other related questions to Inderjit Singh, a four-term MP for the People's Action Party (PAP) from 1996 to 2015. The NCMPs who served during Singh's terms in Parliament were J. B. Jeyaretnam, Steve Chia, Sylvia Lim, Lina Chiam, Gerald Giam and Yee Jenn Jong.

"A 'stabiliser' for our first-past-the-post electoral system"

By Goh Chok Tong

This article was posted on Facebook on 4 July 2020, six days before polling night of the 2020 General Election.[1] Reproduced with kind permission from Emeritus Senior Minister Goh Chok Tong.

Mr Lee Kuan Yew and I were the architects of the NCMP scheme. Let me explain why we mooted it.

Soon after Mr J. B. Jeyaretnam entered Parliament in 1981, Mr Lee watched how the PAP backbenchers ably debated with him. He concluded that it was good for the development of our democracy to have such robust debates on government policies in Parliament. Having opposition MPs also allows the ruling party to debate and debunk issues in Parliament which the opposition would otherwise raise outside. The opposition, too, needs checks-and-balances.

Mr Lee and I never feared having checks-and-balances or alternative voices in Parliament. In fact, it was our wish to guarantee them that led us to create the NCMP scheme.

Compared to other countries, Singapore's constituencies are rather homogeneous, since public housing is spread out across the island. This means it is possible for a party that performs well in a General Election to win all, if not an overwhelming majority, of the seats in Parliament. Indeed, for almost 17 years after independence, Singapore did not have a single opposition MP. It was precisely to prevent this total absence of opposition voices in Parliament that Mr Lee and I decided to establish the NCMP scheme.

We studied other countries' parliamentary systems and discovered that Mauritius had a unique "Best Losers System" to ensure fair representation of its ethnic minorities. In Mauritius's parliament today, in addition to 62 directly-elected MPs, 8 seats go to the best losers from the minority ethnic groups. (For Singapore, the GRC system ensures multi-racial representation in Parliament.)

Similarly, our NCMP system guarantees opposition voices in Parliament. At the same time, it reduces the probability of the ruling party having its mandate significantly weakened, or even being voted out of office, when that is not really what the voters want.

Let's say there's a 60/40 vote share between the ruling and opposition parties. It only takes a swing of 10 percentage points to change the government, intentionally or unintentionally.

If Singaporeans consciously vote to remove the ruling party from government, that is their political right. But if they vote for the opposition to ensure checks-and-balances in Parliament, even though they still want the ruling party to form the government, then an unintended election outcome is entirely possible.

Some people have commented that the intent of the NCMP scheme is to shut out the opposition and entrench the ruling party in power. But the reality is no NCMP scheme would prevent an incompetent, unpopular or corrupt ruling party from being swept out of power — and deservedly so.

As designed, the NCMP scheme acts as a "stabiliser" for our first-past-the-post electoral system. Singapore is a "sampan-sized" country. Its stability was always at the back of Mr Lee's and my minds. Therefore, we decided to secure the sampan with outriggers. Then you can put a sail on the sampan, catch the wind and go fast without fear of it capsizing. The NCMP scheme is an important outrigger for our political system.

I supported PM's move to increase the number of NCMPs from 9 to 12 and to accord them the same voting rights as directly-elected MPs. Like me, he believes that the opposition is necessary as part of a healthy Parliamentary system. He has listened carefully to Singaporeans' wishes

121

for more opposition voices in Parliament. Increasing the number of NCMPs by three and giving them the same voting rights as directly-elected MPs are very significant constitutional changes.

I hope you will now have a better understanding of the fundamental intent of the NCMP scheme. When you vote, you are not only choosing who you want to represent you in Parliament and run your town council, you are also choosing a party to lead and govern Singapore. For this GE, you will be choosing the party to steer our sampan in the midst of the COVID-19 pandemic and other serious domestic and external challenges.

Politics is not a game of poker. The NCMP scheme guarantees that the new Parliament will have at least 12 opposition MPs. It is a winning hand for Singapore's democracy. — gct

An interview with Inderjit Singh

(This interview was conducted on 19 December 2022. The views expressed were the personal views of Inderjit Singh.)

KEY:
IS — Inderjit Singh
LHY — Loke Hoe Yeong
JJ — Yee Jenn Jong

LHY: If we look at the parliamentary speech by Lee Kuan Yew when he introduced the NCMP scheme in 1984, one of the reasons he cited was to give younger PAP ministers and backbenchers the chance to train their debating skills, because they did not have to deal with the PAP's communist opponents of the 1950s and 60s.

From your point of view, did having an opposition presence in Parliament actually influence the way you debate?

IS: I think it definitely did, because for the first time, we had a real, opposite view in Parliament. Among the PAP, we may not have been talking about the same thing, and we did have debates between ourselves — but it was different from having someone who was there to propose completely opposite views. In order to try to lay down an argument to win the debate against the opposition, I think it was important that we learned how to defend our position. Lee Kuan Yew saw that more and more people wanted a PAP government, and at the same time, they also wanted to have some opposition in Parliament. Rather than having them win outright, we said, okay, we let the 'best losers' come in. So I think the dual objectives were to have sparring partners for the PAP, and to let people have their desire of having an opposition in Parliament.

LHY: With all the opposition members you have encountered in Parliament, what is your assessment of them in terms of being sparring partners. Was it what you had expected? Did you wish they were more or less aggressive in their questioning of the government?

IS: I think in many debates, I probably was more aggressive than the opposition. That's just me, compared to other PAP MPs. In some areas, I raised views that may have been contrary to that of the PAP leaders because I really believed that we needed to change ourselves to address some of those issues. So I think not all the opposition MPs were effective in that sense. My sense of some opposition MPs was that Parliament was new to them, and they were trying to find their way around as to what was going to offend the PAP leaders. And so they were a bit more careful. For people like me, the PAP knows us and they have done a thorough check on who we are, and they understand where we're coming from. That's just my assessment throughout my terms in Parliament. Of course, there were good opposition MPs. Low Thia Khiang was very good. He had experience on the ground, and he understood the issues he debated. Then some of the subsequent MPs and NCMPs who came, like Yee Jenn Jong and Gerald Giam, brought very good arguments. They also had a good feel of the ground, and were a bit more measured — compared to J. B. Jeyaretnam in the old days, who just went about opposing everything the PAP did.

LHY: You used to debate J. B. Jeyaretnam in Parliament?

IS: The most prominent one was when he proposed a motion in Parliament about inequality in Singapore. That was what we were facing at that time. I looked at it, and I proposed an amendment to his motion from being very negative to something more constructive. Then Parliament had to vote on the amended motion, and my motion got voted but his was not. If you look at the Hansard report, he basically said that the PAP was not doing anything, and we had an inequality problem. Maybe we cannot deny that. I guess I was the right guy to counter propose. I think there was a problem with inequality. But it didn't mean that we were not doing anything about it. Maybe we could have done more. But his point was that we were doing nothing about it. And so I amended the motion.

We were not confrontational. I think he was upset, and so we had an exchange. There was a real, robust debate, not just with me, but with everyone else, because that was his motion. So that was an example. Later, we had the ministerial salary debate. I thought the Workers' Party [under Low Thia Khiang's leadership] could have been a bit more aggressive. But again, as I said, they thought maybe that's being constructive. That's just my assessment.

JJ: You must be referring to the 2012 debate on ministerial salary.

IS: I thought what the Workers' Party did was just to propose a different version of the PAP's formula. I'm saying that the Workers' Party owes it to their voters to suggest something very radical. But I think that's okay too, to just use the PAP's idea and modify it. That's one way of debating, right? You could have come up with something completely different. That could be what set the stage for the Workers' Party's approach today of being constructive in debates. I would say that was after J. B. Jeyaretnam and maybe also after Lee Siew Choh was NCMP. That was how it was with Chiam See Tong. It was more of that kind of arguments, rather than head-on clashes. So that shaped the type of debates we have had since then.

LHY: I'm wondering about the changes over the years that you have been in Parliament. Do you think PAP backbenchers have gotten more or less combative in debating opposition MPs over the years? What do you think of the current batch of PAP backbenchers? Do you think they are becoming better at pressing the opposition?

IS: If you look at the 4G ministers, I think they are a lot more combative because there are now more opposition MPs. So the debate has become a lot more intense compared to the past, when we did not have that kind of numbers of opposition MPs. But I think among the PAP MPs, I don't see the aggressive debate coming from backbenchers, but more from the Ministers and Ministers of State. That's just my observation.

LHY: Do you think the NCMP scheme backfired for the PAP? I mean, each time the PAP raised the maximum number of NCMP positions, more opposition MPs then got elected outright. Do you think this somehow emboldened Singaporeans to vote for the opposition?

IS: I think this is the effect of the changing psyche of voters. The second is the quality of opposition candidates. I think this is where the NCMP scheme has been very useful for the opposition, or at least for the Workers' Party. Those who came in as NCMPs have been of good quality, like Jenn Jong and Gerald. They were not of the old style of opposition, just opposing the PAP for the sake of opposing. They brought very important arguments. I think all this has had a positive effect in the minds of people, with regard to the opposition. Otherwise, there was no platform for the opposition. So this is where I think it has worked against the PAP.

Naturally the electorate has also shifted, as people want more opposition voices in Parliament. So I don't think the NCMP scheme was contributing to more opposition candidates getting elected, just that they were good candidates. And people realised that if the opposition is capable of bringing in good people — in this case, it is the Workers' Party — who then got more exposure, then they will benefit themselves as the electorate.

LHY: So arguably, the NCMP scheme has helped build up the Workers' Party under the leadership of Low Thia Khiang? They had Sylvia Lim as NCMP, then Yee Jenn Jong and Gerald Giam...

IS: One by one, they got elected.

LHY: So, do you think the NCMP scheme has served its purpose, and it is time to move on?

IS: It is more that we are moving forward [as an electorate], and that the chances of opposition candidates getting elected are higher now. Then the NCMP scheme would have run its course and in future, you actually don't really need this scheme anymore. Let's say now, we have 10 to 12 elected opposition members and we got like another nine or 10, and then we have got quite a substantial number. At the next election, let's say there are 20 opposition MPs elected, which I think is quite a substantial number. I don't think that we want another five NCMPs on top of that. At that point, I think the NCMP scheme would have served its purpose. And there are robust debates right now with the opposition in Parliament, even when the NCMPs are not involved.

Let's say 12 opposition MPs are elected at the next general election. Based on the current rules in the Constitution, no NCMP offers will be made, because the quota of 12 opposition MPs has been met for the purpose of the NCMP scheme. Even though the scheme remains, no NCMP positions will be offered. So keeping this scheme is perhaps not a bad idea. Just leave it there. In the future, the political dynamics could change again, right? There could come a time when there will be fewer opposition MPs. There could also come a time when the PAP could be in the opposition, right? I'm talking about 20 to 30 years down the road. So it's not a bad scheme in my opinion. Why change it?

YJJ: That would generally be the argument to support this scheme, and that was what ESM Goh had called a "stabiliser" for our political system. But what we observe without fail, at every election, is that a significant amount of time would be spent debating about this NCMP scheme. The PAP will say that you don't really need to vote for the opposition, that there will automatically be some opposition in Parliament. And the opposition will say "no, that's not real opposition". This is also the view of some journalists who say that too much time is spent just covering this debate at every election. Given that our election campaign period is typically only eight to nine days, you can't really cover a lot of things after spending a couple of days debating the NCMP scheme.

IS: I don't think this will come up at the next election! (laughter) Let's see. If it does, I'll be surprised. But I think the population now is more educated. They will just vote for who they want. [Deputy Prime Minister] Lawrence Wong said that across the six constituencies where the Workers' Party contested in 2020, the Workers' Party won more votes than the PAP![2] So that is a trend right now. So I don't think there'll be a debate on the NCMP scheme at the next election.

JJ: Which is something I really hope to see as well. Just looking through all general elections in the past, and even at the last one [in 2020], the NCMP issue took quite a bit of airtime.

IS: I doubt it will take up airtime next time, but let's see. I am no longer a PAP MP, so I may not know exactly what the party is thinking, but I think the NCMP scheme has already run its course. The population probably won't buy the arguments for the scheme anymore. We are at a time when voters are looking at the quality of candidates on both sides. There are two things. One is the quality of candidates. The other one is also the party — which opposition party is a serious party? There are many other opposition parties which will probably not stand a good chance of winning seats anyway. There are one or two serious opposition parties with good candidates, and their chances of winning seats are quite high now.

LHY: The NCMP scheme may have thrown up some unintended effects. One of those interesting things has been that before an election, opposition parties and candidates would disavow any interest in the NCMP scheme — because they want to win seats outright. But when they do become the best losers after the election, they generally want to accept NCMP seats as far as possible. The best example here is of course J. B. Jeyaretnam. He criticised the scheme for many years. But when an NCMP seat was actually offered to him, he accepted it. I think it was Tan Cheng Bock — then still a PAP backbencher — who said at that time, "I am surprised. I thought he was a man of principle."[3] So I'm wondering — was this an unintended aim of the PAP to put the opposition in a catch-22 situation?

IS: I really doubt there was such an intention. When the NCMP scheme came out, it was most probably for the reasons we have been discussing. And it was probably unfortunate [that J.B. Jeyaretnam was caught in such a predicament], but that is our system. The fact is that the opposition goes into elections with that given system as set by the Constitution — but they are not in charge and they cannot change the rules. So the opposition has to work within those parameters. But the NCMP scheme was not to make the opposition look bad. I don't think that it was the original intent.

LHY: I find it slightly uncanny that whenever the PAP government raised the maximum number of opposition MPs for the purposes of offering NCMP positions, the opposition then saw some growth in numbers. For example, before the 2011 General Election, that maximum number was raised to nine members, and then Aljunied GRC fell to the opposition. Before the 2020 General Election, it was raised to 12 opposition MPs, then Sengkang GRC fell to the opposition. Is this because of the PAP's read of the ground — that there was this groundswell of support for the opposition — and therefore they thought, let's increase the number of NCMPs that can be offered?

IS: This is hard to say. I think the way the PAP would have done it — if I understand them correctly — is that they would have already done some projections of the votes they would get ahead of a general election. And I think based on that, they may have decided, okay, let's try to minimise our losses. So I think that is probably only what they expect. Even if they did not expect those losses in advance, they could have crunched the numbers from anywhere. Also, I think the times have changed. As I mentioned, the quality of opposition candidates is there, and they are now better organised. Whether you increase the numbers of NCMPs or not, more opposition candidates will win. People are more willing to give the opposition their vote. And of course, you know, there is the branding of particular parties. So let's say you put up a Workers' Party candidate — there would be a better chance of them being elected. And I think in the case of West Coast GRC, it was the Tan Cheng Bock brand [which brought the opposition within just two percentage points of winning]. It could have been East Coast gone to opposition, West Coast gone to the opposition, and no NCMP seats offered! Those just happened to be the circumstances.

LHY: You're saying that the PAP did projections of the votes they would get?

IS: They must have done the projections.

LHY: So would you say that the PAP was very surprised at the 2011 and 2020 results, when those GRCs fell?

IS: Of course they were surprised.

LHY: Does it mean that the PAP was mentally prepared for nine opposition MPs in 2011, and 12 opposition MPs in 2020?

IS: I think they were looking at that. You see, for Aljunied GRC in 2011, they had George Yeo, Lim Hwee Hua, Zainul Abidin Rasheed, Ong Ye Kung — four ministers [or in the case of Ong Ye Kung, a potential minister]. I don't think they wanted to lose like that. So they did not expect it. They expected some erosion of their vote, but they did not expect it to swing the other way. The same thing, I think, in 2020, there were many factors. There were some sympathy votes for the opposition, there was unhappiness over cost-of-living issues, and over the way the PAP attacked some opposition candidates — maybe people didn't like what they did to Raeesah Khan [of the Workers' Party] in Sengkang GRC. There were multiple factors which meant we lost votes.

LHY: Is there any sense among PAP MPs of unfairness with regard to the NCMP? You know, that PAP candidates work hard to walk the ground to win, but then the 'best losers' in the opposition get to go into Parliament. Losing PAP candidates don't. Perhaps this may be accentuated now that the rules have been amended for NCMPs to have full voting rights.

IS: No. I've never sensed that in my 20 years in Parliament. There was no feeling of "No, it is not fair". I think [Tan] Cheng Bock probably felt that way when the scheme was first started, and also with the NMP scheme. I think he was not happy. But for the rest of us, I don't think we ever felt that way. We understood that this is the system in place. And I know they have a role to play as part of our Constitution.

YJJ: If I may sum up your views about the NCMP scheme — you are saying that there is no harm in keeping it. The electorate is getting more educated. There are some good opposition members available right now. The chances are that there may not even be any NCMPs at the next election. So there's no need to abolish the scheme, because it's just like an insurance scheme.

IS: That's right, I think there's nothing wrong with it — in case there is a freak election like in the year Lee Kuan Yew passed away, and the opposition saw shock losses. So in 2015, it was very useful to have the NCMP scheme, wasn't it? We will never know. So I think the opposition should not take it for granted. Since we have the NCMP scheme, there's no harm having it there, and no point taking it out. You also don't have to reintroduce the NCMP scheme if you suddenly realise that Singapore needs it.

LHY: Thank you Inderjit. Is there anything else you wanted to raise?

IS: I think we've discussed everything. But I think we should be a bit careful about saying that every time we increase the maximum number of NCMPs, more opposition candidates get elected. I think it is just the circumstances and timing. In 2011, there were many issues. You know, in 2011, I predicted that score.

LHY: Based on your reading of the ground?

IS: Yes, there was an issue of reading the ground by the party's leaders. When they wanted to have that one then, some of us felt that it was the wrong timing — don't do it. So that was a misreading of the ground then. And then Low Thia Khiang made his sudden move in 2011 [to leave his stronghold of Hougang to lead his Aljunied GRC team]. They could have moved our candidates also but they were quite confident. So that was, I think, a wrong understanding of the ground.

The 2015 results surprised everyone. The Workers' Party got very worried that they might lose everything, right? That was a special event. Even for the PAP. We did not expect it to happen.

And 2020 was a very difficult year with the Covid-19 pandemic. When we called for the election, the PAP were actually not doing a great job at that point. There was a sense among Singaporeans that we kept changing the rules during the pandemic. People were wondering — we're supposed to be world-class, but no longer seemed to be so. Many of us felt it was the wrong timing for an election. But now when you look back, the government stabilised things later. Had we waited one year later — or one-and-a-half years later — before calling an election, I think the results would have been quite different.

9

Conclusion
The NCMP Scheme Has
Had Its Time

Loke Hoe Yeong & Yee Jenn Jong

Four decades have elapsed since the Non-Constituency Member of Parliament (NCMP) scheme was introduced in 1984. It remains an issue that is raised and debated at every general election. Yet Singapore's political landscape has seen major changes since the scheme was introduced.

Every seat was contested at the two most recent general elections in 2020 and 2015 which, until then, had never been the case since independence. The opposition has been on a trajectory of gaining more seats and votes with each successive general election, including in GRCs which were once deemed impenetrable — with the notable exception of the 2015 General Election. We would argue that the People Action Party's (PAP) strong results in 2015 were most likely the result of an exceptional set of circumstances related to the SG50 celebrations that year and the passing of Lee Kuan Yew, which will not be repeated.

Is the NCMP scheme therefore living on borrowed time? Is it still useful or meaningful for Singapore to continue with it?

In his chapter in this book, Walter Woon has argued that Singapore's electoral system has evolved to suit the nation's needs, values and culture, and that NCMPs are an important part of that system. He has offered a convincing rebuttal of the fallacy that NCMPs are not the true representatives of the people, just because NCMPs do not win their seats under the first-past-the-post system.

For Steve Chia, the former NCMP then from the National Solidarity Party, the risk of having zero elected opposition MPs in a general election should never be discounted. The NCMP scheme helps guard against this calamitous scenario, however remote. Leong Mun Wai and Hazel Poa, the present NCMPs from the Progress Singapore Party, have found the scheme useful but suggested replacing it with a proportional representation system of democracy to better reflect the wishes of the electorate. Dr Paul Tambyah of the Singapore Democratic Party believes an overhaul of our democratic processes is more important than the NCMP scheme, though this position remains an option for opposition candidates. Similarly, the Workers' Party, with the most NCMPs since the formation of the scheme, has consistently argued against the scheme, preferring a revamp of the Group Representation Constituency (GRC) system and the elections department. The party however, remains open to its members accepting NCMP positions. Likewise, Leon Perera, the former WP NCMP and MP, would rather see unfair political mechanisms being dismantled but opined that with Singapore's unlevel political playing field, opposition parties do not have the luxury of declining NCMP seats on grounds of principle.

Political observers interviewed are supportive of retaining the scheme. Walid Jumblatt Bin Abdullah, Elvin Ong and Eugene Tan all felt the scheme has been useful. Ong suggested increasing the positions to 20% that of elected parliamentarians. He also advocates moving to a hybrid model with proportional representation. Tan proposes a sunset clause which would automatically abolish the scheme once the opposition wins a critical mass of one-third of parliamentary seats, along with other amendments. However, veteran journalist PN Balji calls the NCMP scheme a "quirk" in Singapore's political system and a "sneaky way" to persuade Singaporeans to vote for the PAP. He advocates for the scheme to be scrapped.

Former Prime Minister Goh Chok Tong, a co-designer of the scheme, has likened it to an insurance scheme for our democracy. Meanwhile, Inderjit Singh, the former PAP MP, cautions against the assumption that the opposition's numbers in Parliament will keep growing. In any case, the NCMP scheme does not have to kick in if the opposition surpasses the quota of NCMP seat offers — currently 12 — at each general election.

The NCMP scheme would appear to have been beneficial for the opposition as a whole. It has helped showcase candidates and talents from the opposition in a parliamentary setting, where the stringent first-past-the-post system means that many good, deserving opposition candidates may otherwise never get an airing aside from an electoral campaign.

Indeed, a number of opposition politicians we interviewed are broadly in favour of the NCMP scheme, or shifting to a proportional representation system that would guarantee opposition voices in Parliament. However, what they really want is a more level playing field for opposition parties.

We believe the time has come for the NCMP scheme to be abolished. We make this call as a result of looking at the historical developments behind the scheme, and the arguments for and against it. We do so in the spirit of advocating for a new phase of Singapore's political development, without fear or favour to one or the other side of the political divide. The mindsets of voters have changed, and they are more willing to accept the opposition and even vote them into GRCs. It is time for the 'training wheels' to be taken off so that we can progress towards a mature democracy, and it would be unhealthy to keep relying on the NCMP scheme to ensure opposition representation in Parliament.

Here, we present four key reasons for abolishing the NCMP scheme.

1.   What the opposition really wants is a level playing field.

The NCMP scheme was introduced because of the paltry opposition presence in Parliament in the past. If we were to superficially compare Singapore with most advanced economies in the world, the opposition's presence in Parliament is paltry today as well. We need to see this in the context of the unfair playing field faced by opposition parties and their candidates.

In the 1950s through to the 80s, the PAP government's use of the Internal Security Act to detain opposition politicians without trial decimated their numbers in Parliament,[1] and deterred potential opposition candidates from stepping forward. Then came a period when libel suits brought by PAP leaders against opposition figures had the same effect.

In the relatively more benign political climate in Singapore today, the opposition has highlighted the barriers they continue to face. They have cried foul over gerrymandering where electoral boundaries change much more drastically and frequently than in democracies around the world; constituencies which are nearly won by the opposition have often "disappeared" at the next election, such as when they are merged with neighbouring GRCs.[2] The time gap between the update of electoral boundaries and the general election is often tight too. Elected MPs from the opposition say they face "double standards" in how the People's Association and grassroots groups operate in opposition constituencies, even as they carry out their municipal responsibilities.[3] They have also complained of unfair coverage by the mainstream media, as well as the restrictions posed by the Protection from Online Falsehoods and Manipulation Act.

Cynics charge that the NCMP scheme exists simply to make the PAP "look good". While the PAP — just like any ruling party in the world — wants to win as many seats as possible and retain power, it is not in its interest either to have zero opposition representation in Parliament today. That would make the PAP look more authoritarian and repressive than it actually intends to be, to domestic as well as international audiences — which would be to its own reputational detriment. The NCMP scheme helps the PAP guarantee some opposition presence in Parliament.

While successive PAP leaders have said it is not their duty or responsibility to help the opposition get elected, having a fairer playing field for the opposition would help the PAP build trust with voters. This would come at a time when Singaporeans — younger voters in particular — are speaking up more.

We believe that the Singapore electorate no longer wants token opposition representation in Parliament. There has been a steady growth in votes and seats for the opposition over the decades, in spite of the NCMP scheme and its expansion. Also, voters in Singapore have shown to be particularly astute all along — it has often been cited how opposition sympathisers in the by-elections in Anson in 1981, and in Punggol East in 2013, have carefully avoided splitting the opposition vote when there were three- or four-cornered fights, thus delivering victory to the strongest opposition candidate. Even with the remote possibility of an opposition wipeout at a general election, we believe that there will be a natural electoral response at the subsequent general election to correct the situation.

2.   Too much time and press are "wasted" on arguments about the NCMP scheme every general election.

At every general election since 1984, the PAP has made the argument in some form that voters should feel free to vote for their candidates, as the NCMP scheme guarantees a minimum number of opposition MPs. They do so with the knowledge that there is probably a sizeable number of voters who want more opposition voices in Parliament, but who also want a PAP government ultimately for the time being. Opposition parties then often respond that NCMPs — by the nature of their role — cannot be true representatives of the people, thereby urging Singaporeans to vote freely for the opposition if they want to be heard. Some opposition candidates find themselves having to hedge their responses, in the event that they are offered an NCMP seat and would like to keep open the option of accepting the seat.

The essence of this debate over NCMPs has been repeated at every general election since 1984. While it is not exactly a negative thing, we believe that this does not make for a meaningful political debate. When the PAP invokes the NCMP scheme during elections, it seems to be saying to voters: Even if you don't like the policies we are proposing in this campaign, there will always be a guaranteed number of opposition MPs to speak up for you. Should elections not be about a party seeking a mandate for its policy prescriptions and thus form the government?

Again, cynics charge that the PAP knows the NCMP scheme works in some way to its advantage — namely in keeping the growth of the opposition in check, lest voters are emboldened to vote for more and more opposition into Parliament. That is why, these cynics charge that the PAP has decided to keep the NCMP scheme.

In speaking to figures from both the PAP and most of the opposition parties though, we had the distinct sense that this is not how voters — whom they regularly encounter on the ground — process in their minds the choice to be made at each election. Put another way, our interviewees from both sides of the political divide do not believe that if the NCMP scheme were to be abolished tomorrow, more voters would start voting more boldly for the opposition. It is therefore not likely that narrow-minded tactical advantage is the reason for the PAP government to retain the NCMP scheme. The PAP does really see the NCMP scheme as an insurance scheme for democracy, as Goh Chok Tong put it, in the event of a complete wipeout of the opposition from Parliament, which the PAP does not even want.

Some of our interviewees did not find it to be an issue that arguments about the NCMP scheme were rehashed at every general election since 1984. Nevertheless, we do not believe these arguments have added any value to the election campaigns of either the PAP or the opposition.

3. **The rules for offering NCMP seats can seem arbitrary, and the spirit behind the scheme comes across as being contradictory. This could damage political trust and the principles of democracy.** The conclusion of Chapter 2 of this book raised questions on aspects of how the NCMP scheme has operated which seem arbitrary. The Parliamentary Elections Act does not lay down the number of alternative offers of NCMP positions that must be made, if there are NCMPs who decline each offer made to them. As suggested by former Nominated Member of Parliament Eugene Tan, there can be clearer rules spelled out as to how many further seats may be offered in the event of that initial offers of NCMP seats are rejected.

In the year which could have seen the pioneering use of the NCMP scheme (1984), it was decided not to make further offers of the NCMP position after M.P.D. Nair and Tan Chee Kien declined it. This was so even though the minimum threshold required to be offered an NCMP position was set at a low 15% of the vote in a constituency — and yet a significant number of other candidates scored well above 40% in the 1984 General Election.

Opposition candidates are also caught in a situation of 'damned if you do, damned if you don't' when they are offered NCMP seats. The PAP sometimes castigates them when they ultimately accept an NCMP seat, especially if they or their party may have criticised the NCMP scheme in some way during the election campaign — although this phenomenon has been on the wane since the days of J. B. Jeyaretnam. On the other hand, the PAP also castigates them if they do not accept the offer of an NCMP seat, as Lee Li Lian and the Workers' Party found out to their exasperation, when Lee declined the NCMP seat and her party sought to 'transfer' the offer to Daniel Goh in 2016. Lee was caught in a catch-22 situation when Chan Chun Sing, then Minister in the Prime Minister's Office, said it was "regrettable" that she had chosen to "reject her NCMP seat and with that her responsibility to her voters and Singapore".[4] (We cover this incident in Chapter 2 of the book.)

Some cynics believe that the PAP devised the NCMP scheme to bind opposition candidates in a trap, while making a show of 'guaranteeing' an opposition presence in Parliament. Again, our interviews with both PAP and opposition politicians for this book indicate no such sentiments among them. Nevertheless, this is unhealthy for the purpose of building trust with voters as regards Singapore's electoral system.

4. It is time to move on from the legacy of the 1980s.

Forty years after the NCMP scheme was introduced, Singapore's political scene has changed. While the number of elected opposition MPs is still small (about 10% of Parliament currently) by the standard of democratic societies worldwide, the opposition has shown that it can win seats outright even in GRCs which were thought to be impregnable for the PAP.

Over the past two decades, better qualified candidates have joined the opposition. They have also shown that the doomsday scenario painted by the PAP of opposition-run constituencies with 'rubbish piled three storeys high' — ostensibly because opposition politicians presumed to be such poor municipal managers — has not materialised. After some initial hiccups, due in part to the lack of access to the town council management information system, town councils run by the opposition have scored comparably to those managed by the PAP, in the annual town council management report released by the Ministry of National Development.

It may still be too early to say that the opposition has grown sufficiently to take on the PAP and win enough seats to have a critical mass of voices in Parliament. Nevertheless, we feel that it is unhealthy to continue to rely on schemes like that for NCMPs and Nominated Members of Parliament to be the alternative voices to the PAP. Now is time to seriously relook the legacy political structures set up in the 1980s and in their place, establish fairer and more universally accepted democratic processes — to build a truly "democratic society based on justice and equality" as envisaged by S. Rajaratnam in our National Pledge.

Conclusion

Singapore has been holding elections for more than seven decades now. It is time to move forward with our democratic development. We believe the time has come to do away with the NCMP scheme, together with rectifications to the mesh of other electoral measures introduced by the PAP in the 1980s, to correct an unfavourable political situation.

We make this recommendation in the bipartisan spirit of securing the best for Singapore in its long-term political development. Our democracy should be allowed to power forward towards a 'First-World Parliament' — as the Workers' Party put it in its 2011 election manifesto — without being held back by legacy structures that attempt to mask the inadequacies of our system. And with its own moves such as in officially recognising a Leader of the Opposition after the 2020 General Election, we believe the PAP leaders are also prepared to take Singapore's democracy forward.

Appendix
Profiles of the NCMPs

Loke Hoe Yeong

Lee Siew Choh (1917–2002)

NCMP term: 1988–1991
Party: The Workers' Party

Dr Lee Siew Choh led the Barisan Sosialis party as its founding chairman, after he and his fellow legislative assemblymen split with the People's Action Party (PAP) in 1961. A doctor by training, Lee was the legislative assemblyman for Queenstown and parliamentary secretary to the minister for home affairs during his time with the PAP.

Under Lee's leadership, Barisan Sosialis boycotted Singapore's first parliamentary session in 1965, as well as Singapore's first general election after independence.

In 1988, Barisan Sosialis merged with the Workers' Party (WP), and Lee contested as a WP candidate in Eunos Group Representation Constituency (GRC). He became one of Singapore's first two Non-Constituency Members of Parliament (NCMPs), the other being Francis Seow who was disqualified from taking up his seat in Parliament. Lee resigned from the WP in 1993.

J. B. Jeyaretnam (1926–2008)

NCMP term: 1997–2001
Party: The Workers' Party

Joshua Benjamin Jeyaretnam served as a magistrate, crown counsel, deputy public prosecutor and registrar of the Supreme Court in the 1950s and 60s. In 1971, he was elected as the secretary-general of the WP, which had been dormant after its founder, David Marshall, left the party.

After five failed attempts to get elected, he finally became the first opposition MP after Singapore's independence, when he won the Anson by-election of 1981. He was reelected at the 1984 General Election, but was disqualified from Parliament after being fined S$5,000 for making a false declaration in the WP accounts — which Jeyaretnam denied.

Jeyaretnam reentered Parliament in 1997 as an NCMP, after his performance as the 'best loser' in the hotly contested Cheng San GRC during that election. He was again disqualified from Parliament before the end of his term, when he was declared bankrupt as a result of lawsuits by the PAP leaders. He subsequently established a new party — the Reform Party — but died before he could contest in an election again.

Steve Chia (b. 1970)

NCMP term: 2001–2006
Party: National Solidarity Party/Singapore Democratic Alliance

Steve Chia Khiah Hong, a remisier, joined the National Solidarity Party (NSP) in 1995, having been active in university student politics. He became secretary-general of the NSP in 2001, and went on to become an NCMP later that year, when he emerged as that election's 'best loser' in Chua Chu Kang Single Member Constituency (SMC). The NSP contested the 2001 General Election as a member of the Singapore Democratic Alliance.

Chia later left the NSP to join the Singapore People's Party (SPP), of which he became the secretary-general in 2019.

Sylvia Lim (b. 1965)

NCMP term: 2006–2011
Party: The Workers' Party

Sylvia Lim Swee Lian has been the chairman of the WP since 2003. A lawyer by profession, she became an NCMP in 2006 when her Aljunied GRC team emerged as the 'best loser' in that election. In 2011, she re-contested Aljunied GRC, which became the first GRC to be won by the opposition. It also meant that she became the first NCMP to be successfully elected outright at a subsequent election.

Lim was reelected as an MP for Aljunied GRC in 2015 and 2020. Before entering politics, Lim served in the Singapore Police Force and was then a law lecturer at Temasek Polytechnic.

Lina Chiam (b. 1949)

NCMP term: 2011–2015
Party: Singapore People's Party

A UK-trained nurse, Lina Loh Woon Lee — known publicly as Lina Chiam — was a founding member of the Singapore Democratic Party and the SPP along with her husband, the veteran opposition politician Chiam See Tong. She served as a town councillor for Potong Pasir Town Council from 1984 to 2011.

She made her electoral debut at the 2011 General Election when she contested in Potong Pasir, the constituency of which Chiam See Tong was MP for 27 years. She became an NCMP when she lost the contest by only 114 votes, but managed to score the highest votes among the opposition candidate 'losers'. She contested unsuccessfully in Potong Pasir again in 2015. She was chairman of the SPP from 2012 to 2019.

Yee Jenn Jong (b. 1965)

NCMP term: 2011–2015
Party: The Workers' Party

Yee Jenn Jong joined the WP in 2011 and contested in Joo Chiat SMC. He was co-opted into WP's Central Executive Committee (CEC) after becoming an NCMP and served in the CEC until 2016, taking roles as assistant treasurer, treasurer and webmaster separately during that period. He contested in Marine Parade GRC in 2015 after Joo Chiat SMC was merged with that GRC, and again in the same GRC in 2020.

Yee is an entrepreneur and book author, including authoring the book *Journey in Blue: A Peek into the Workers' Party of Singapore*, detailing his time with the WP. He remains a member of the WP at this time of writing.

Gerald Giam (b. 1977)

NCMP term: 2011–2015
Party: The Workers' Party

Gerald Giam Yean Song contested in East Coast GRC in 2011, and became an NCMP. He recontested that GRC in 2015 — while his team was eligible to accept one NCMP position, he proposed for his team mate Leon Perera to take up the offer in his place.

Giam contested in Aljunied GRC in 2020 and won, returning to Parliament as an MP. He is the head of policy research of the WP and the vice-chairman of Aljunied-Hougang Town Council at this time of writing.

He is the chief technology officer of an IT solutions company which he co-founded. He served as a foreign service officer at the Ministry of Foreign Affairs, and was formerly a deputy editor at *The Online Citizen*.

Dennis Tan (b. 1970)

NCMP term: 2015–2020
Party: The Workers' Party

Dennis Tan Lip Fong joined the WP in 2012, and has been the party's organising secretary since 2018. He contested in Fengshan SMC in 2015 and became an NCMP. In 2020, he contested in Hougang SMC and won.

Tan has practised as a shipping lawyer since 1997, including a stint in an English law firm. He is currently a partner at a shipping law firm, DennisMathiew, which he co-founded.

Leon Perera (b. 1970)

NCMP term: 2015–2020
Party: The Workers' Party

Leon Perera contested in East Coast GRC in the 2015 General Election and became an NCMP in the 2016–2020 parliamentary term. Prior to politics, he worked in the public sector, private sector as well as in volunteerism and activism. He co-founded an international research consultancy and served as its CEO and then Chairman.

He contested in Aljunied GRC in 2020 and won, returning to Parliament as an MP. He was head of the WP's media team, as well as the vice-chairman of the Aljunied-Hougang Town Council, until he resigned as an MP in 2023.

Daniel Goh (b. 1973)

NCMP term: 2015–2020
Party: The Workers' Party

Associate Professor Daniel Goh Pei Siong is a sociologist at the faculty of the National University of Singapore (NUS). At this time of writing, he is vice dean (special programmes) at NUS College, and is associate provost (undergraduate education).

He contested in East Coast GRC in 2015, and became an NCMP when he filled the NCMP seat which was declined by Lee Li Lian who contested in Punggol East SMC. He did not contest in the 2020 General Election and has since retired from politics.

Leong Mun Wai (b. 1959)

NCMP term: 2020–
Party: Progress Singapore Party

Leong Mun Wai is a CEC member of the Progress Singapore Party (PSP) and its secretary-general from April 2023 to February 2024. He contested in West Coast GRC in 2020, and became one of two NCMPs from that team.

Leong was managing director of OCBC Securities, director of Merrill Lynch Hong Kong, and investment officer of Government of Singapore Investment Corporation. He is currently CEO of Timbre Capital, the private equity firm he founded.

Hazel Poa (b. 1970)

NCMP term: 2020–
Party: Progress Singapore Party

Hazel Poa Koon Koon is the secretary-general of the PSP. She contested in West Coast GRC in 2020, and became one of two NCMPs from that team.

She had previously contested in a general election as a member of the NSP, of which she was secretary-general from 2011 to 2013. She joined the PSP in 2019.

Poa served in the Singapore Civil Service in the Administrative Service upon her graduation from the University of Cambridge. She then worked in the finance sector before starting a chain of private education entities with her husband.

Offered the NCMP role, but who rejected it or did not serve

M.P.D. Nair (1920–1989)

Offered NCMP position in: 1984

During the 1950s, Madai Puthan Damodaran Nair was minister of communications and works in Lim Yew Hock's government, and was assistant minister to the chief secretary in David Marshall's government. After Lim Yew Hock lost to Lee Kuan Yew and the PAP in the 1959 General Election, he studied law in London, becoming a lawyer upon his return to Singapore.

He joined the WP when J. B. Jeyaretnam became its new leader in the 1970s. M.P.D. Nair contested in Jalan Kayu in 1984, where he polled 48.8%, which was the 'best loser' performance in that election, thus becoming the first person to have been offered an NCMP position — which he did not take up, because the CEC of the WP voted to reject the seat in objection to the NCMP scheme.

Tan Chee Kien (b. 1956)

Offered NCMP position in: 1984

Tan Chee Kien, a businessman, was chairman of the Singapore United Front when he contested in Kaki Bukit in 1984 and polled 47.8%. He was offered an NCMP position after the WP decided to decline the offer initially put to them — but Tan also declined the offer in objection to the NCMP scheme.

He then left the Singapore United Front to join the NSP, under whose banner he contested in elections until 2011.

Francis Seow (1928–2016)

Offered NCMP position in: 1988 (disqualified before taking his seat)

Francis Seow Tiang Siew was the solicitor-general from 1969 to 1972, after which he went into private practice. He was elected president of the Law Society of Singapore in 1986.

In the 1988 General Election, Seow joined the WP and contested in Eunos GRC, losing with 49.11% of the vote. Offers of two NCMP positions were made to the WP Eunos GRC team, one of which Seow accepted.

Later that year however, Seow was convicted in absentia of tax evasion and fined. He was thus disqualified from being an NCMP. He lived in exile in the US until he died in 2016.

Lee Li Lian (b. 1978)

Offered NCMP position in: 2015

Lee Li Lian, then a financial trainer, won the Punggol East SMC by-election of 2013 in a four-cornered fight — her second attempt at winning that constituency. After serving as an MP for two years, she narrowly lost her seat at the 2015 General Election. She declined the offer of an NCMP position.

At this time of writing, she is chairman of the audit committee for Sengkang Town Council and remains a member of the WP.

Endnotes

Preface

1. Reuters, "No party has monopoly on power, says Singapore PM, week after surprise Malaysia election", 16 May 2018. https://www.reuters.com/article/us-singapore-politics-idUSKCN1IH21Y

Chapter 1

1. Elections Department Singapore Parliamentary General Elections Results, https://www.eld.gov.sg/elections_past_parliamentary.html
2. Singapore Parliamentary Reports, Vol 44 col 1722, 24 July 1984.
3. Ibid, col 1726.
4. Ibid, cols 1727–1729.
5. Ibid, col 1834.
6. Despite Lee's scathing assessment of Jeyaretnam, it should be noted that in the subsequent 1984 General Election he won Anson with 56.81% of the vote. Elections Department Singapore Parliamentary General Elections Results https://www.eld.gov.sg/elections_past_parliamentary.html. By 1988 General Election, Anson had disappeared as a constituency and Jeyaretnam did not stand for election.
7. For the sake of transparency, I declare that I was one of those; I did not vote for the PAP in the 1980 General Election.
8. Ibid, col 1754.
9. Constitution of the Republic of Singapore, art 39(1)(b).
10. Constitution of the Republic of Singapore (Amendment) Act 2016, No 28 of 2016. In force 1 April 2017.

11. UK Election Statistics: 1918–2022, A Long Century of Elections (Richard Cracknell, Elise Uberoi, Mathew Burton; House of Commons Library Research Briefing, 5 December 2022), at p7.
12. Ibid, p8.
13. In the 1929, 1951 and 1974 General Elections. Ibid, p7.
14. Ibid, pp11–12.
15. Ibid, p7.
16. Ibid, p29.
17. This in fact happened twice pre-Independence. In 1957 Soh Ghee Soon of the Liberal Socialist Party won the Cairnhill by-election with 40.28%. David Marshall of the WP won the Anson by-election in 1961, obtaining 43.32%. See the Elections Department Singapore Parliamentary General Elections Results, https://www.eld.gov.sg/elections_past_parliamentary.html.
18. Elections Department Singapore Parliamentary General Elections Results, https://www.eld.gov.sg/elections_past_results.html. For the record, I voted for Dr Tony Tan.
19. See the website of the Bundestagswahlleiter (Federal Returning Officer) at https://bundeswahlleiter.de/en/bundestagswahlen/2021/wahlkreiseinteilung.html.
20. See The German Bundestag — Functions and Procedures (Susanne Linn and Frank Sobolewski; Kürschners Politikkontakte, Germany, 2015), pp9–10 for an explanation of the composition of the Bundestag. Accessible at https://www.btg-bestellservice.de/pdf/80080000.pdf.
21. See the website of the Bundestagswahlleiter (Federal Returning Officer) at https://bundeswahlleiter.de/en/bundestagswahlen/2021/gewaehlte/bund-99/land-9.html.

Chapter 2

1. Lim Puay Ling, Non-Constituency Member of Parliament (NCMP) scheme, Singapore Infopedia, 2016. https://eresources.nlb.gov.sg/infopedia/articles/SIP_1743_2010-12-24.html
2. Lee Kuan Yew, in Singapore Parliamentary Reports, Vol 44 col 1723, 24 July 1984.

3. Subhas Anandan, It's Easy to Cry (Singapore: Marshall Cavendish Editions, 2015), 105–6.
4. 'Reject non-constituency MP seat' call by SUF, The Straits Times, 27 December 1984.
5. Police show mug shots to SUF chief, The Straits Times, 19 January 1985.
6. Loke Hoe Yeong, The First Wave: JBJ, Chiam & the Opposition in Singapore (Singapore: Epigram, 2019), 140–4.
7. Francis Seow claims he has been denied seat in Parliament, Business Times, 7 January 1989.
8. Place for never-say-die critics like Siew Choh, The Straits Times, 21 October 1990.
9. PM leaves for Hongkong today, en route to China, The Straits Times, 14 October 1990.
10. No office for Siew Choh, The Straits Times, 17 March 1989.
11. Workers' Party may boycott first presidential election: Siew Choh, The Straits Times, 3 August 1991.
12. Siew Choh quits, New Paper, 6 August 1993.
13. WP's Cheng San team offered one NCMP seat, The Straits Times, 10 January 1997.
14. Jeyaretnam says 'yes' to offer of NCMP seat, The Straits Times, 11 January 1997.
15. Place for never-say-die critics like Siew Choh, The Straits Times, 21 October 1990.
16. Expect the same old JBJ, The New Paper, 28 January 1997.
17. NCMP scheme achieved little, should be scrapped, The Straits Times, 18 January 1997.
18. Wong Kan Seng in Singapore Parliamentary Reports, Vol 87 col 56, 26 April 2010.
19. Eric Tan a 'friend and mentor': WP's Giam, TODAY, 14 May 2011.
20. Written interview with Eric Tan, December 2023.
21. Ibid.
22. Lee Hsien Loong in Singapore Parliamentary Reports, Vol 94, 27 January 2016.

23. GE2020: PSP's Leong Mun Wai will reject NCMP seat if offered, proposes proportional representation, Yahoo! News, 4 July 2020. https://sg.news.yahoo.com/ge-2020-ps-ps-leong-mun-wai-will-reject-ncmp-seat-if-offered-proposes-proportional-representation-063933854.html

24. PSP's Leong Mun Wai and Hazel Poa step down from party positions to focus on NCMP duties, The Straits Times, 20 July 2020. https://www.straitstimes.com/politics/psps-leong-mun-wai-and-hazel-poa-step-down-from-party-positions-to-focus-on-ncmp-duties

25. Interview with Yee Jenn Jong, Ng Wai Mun and the author, June 2023.

26. Ibid.

27. Singapore Parliamentary Reports, Vol 94, 29 January 2016.

28. NCMPs — Govt's answer to need for an opposition, The Straits Times, 6 September 1988.

29. Lee Kuan Yew in Singapore Parliamentary Reports, Vol 44 col 1723, 24 July 1984.

Chapter 3

1. The NCMP scheme then had set the maximum number of NCMPs at six. However, the actual number of NCMPs that could be declared elected at any general election was fixed at three. The President, acting on the advice of the Cabinet, could order that between four and six NCMPs be declared elected for the purpose of a particular general election. However, from 1984 till 2010 when the number was raised to a minimum of nine, there had never been any presidential order to increase beyond three.

2. On 1 July 2010, the need for a presidential order to increase the number of NCMPs was removed. The maximum number of NCMPs in Parliament was increased from six to nine.

3. On 9 November 2016, a bill to amend the Constitution was passed to increase the maximum number of NCMPs from nine to 12, and to confer upon NCMPs the same voting powers as elected MPs. The procedure for electing up to 12 NCMPs after a general election was brought into effect on 2 January 2019.

4. PAP at turning point again, next 35 years will be quite different from the last: PM Lee, The Straits Times, 14 December 2021.

5. The Constitution of the Republic of Singapore (Amendment) Act 2010 (No. 9 of 2010) and the Parliamentary Elections (Amendment) Act 2010 (No. 16 of 2010), both of which came in force on 1 July 2010.

6. See second reading speech by DPM Wong Kan Seng on the Constitution of the Republic of Singapore (Amendment) Bill, https://www.mlaw.gov.sg/news/parliamentary-speeches/second-reading-speech-by-dpm-wong-kan-seng-on-the-constitution-of-the-republic-of-singapore/

7. SPP — Chiam See Tong "not interested" in NCMP position, TODAYonline, 27 April 2011, https://www.youtube.com/watch?v=ipCtXC-9_gE

8. Some unhappiness on the ground included high public housing costs, huge influx of foreigners, public transport and public health care system unable to cope with the increasing population, and rising income inequality. See for instance: Kevin Y.L. Tan and Terence Lee, Voting in Change: The Politics of Singapore's 2011 General Election (Singapore: Ethos Books, 2011).

9. NCMPs add to voices in Parliament, says PM, The Straits Times, 13 April 2011.

10. PM Lee Hsien Loong: NCMPs to get equal voting rights as MPs; opposition MPs to increase from 9 to 12 next GE, The Straits Times, 27 January 2016.

11. Relevant changes to the Presidential Election that prevented Dr Tan Cheng Bock from contesting again:

    1. A presidential election will be reserved for a community if no person belonging to that community has held the office of President for any of the five most recent terms of office of the President.

    2. President Wee Kim Wee is considered to have served the first elected presidential term in Singapore. As he and the three subsequent holders of the office of President (with S. R. Nathan serving two terms) belong to the Chinese or Indian communities, the 2017 Presidential Election was reserved for a member of the Malay community.

    3. A prospective candidate has to submit a community declaration, which will state the community that an applicant considers himself to be a member of, to the newly constituted Community Committee.

    4. Prospective applicants from the private sector has been tightened significantly. Previously, an individual who had served as the chairman

or chief executive officer of a company with at least S$100 million in paid-up capital could run for President. Now, an individual from the private sector seeking to run for office is required to have experience and ability comparable to that of a chief executive of a company with S$500 million in shareholders' equity for his most recent three-year period of service as chief executive. The company that he or she helmed must have made profit after tax for the entire period that he or she served as the chief executive.

Source: Victor Looi, All You Need to Know About the Changes to Singapore's Presidential Elections 2017, Singapore Legal Advice, 2017, https://singaporelegaladvice.com/changes-singapore-presidential-elections-2017

Chapter 4

1. Bertha Henson, Comment: The NCMP scheme is good for who exactly, Yahoo! News, 2 July 2020, https://sg.news.yahoo.com/comment-the-ncmp-scheme-is-good-for-who-exactly-010203716.html
2. Derek da Cunha, Breakthrough 2.0: Singaporeans Push for Parliamentary Democracy (Singapore: World Scientific Publishing, 2022).
3. Elias Dinas, Pedro Riera and Nasos Roussias (2014). Staying in the First League: Parliamentary Representation and the Electoral Success of Small Parties, Political Science Research and Methods, 3(2), 187–204.
4. Heng Swee Keat, What does WP really want?, People's Action Party, 2020. https://www.pap.org.sg/news/ge2020-news/hsk-ncmp-0507/
5. Chong Zhi Liang, WP files motion to have NCMP seat offered to Lee Li Lian declared vacant; wants Daniel Goh to take it up, The Straits Times, 18 January 2016.
6. Sylvia Lim, Motion on NCMP seat, Workers' Party. https://www.wp.sg/motion-on-ncmp-seat-speech-by-sylvia-lim/
7. Justin Ong, WP's Daniel Goh will not contest next GE for health reasons, 21, TODAYonline, 21 April 2020, https://www.todayonline.com/singapore/wps-daniel-goh-will-not-contest-upcoming-ge-health-reasons
8. Bilveer Singh, Walid Jumblatt Abdullah, and Felix Tan, Unmasking Singapore's 2020 General Elections: COVID-19 and the Evolving Political Landscape (Singapore: World Scientific Publishing, 2021).

9. Nigel Chua, Why SPP's Steve Chia still running race despite losing 4 elections: 'I want to make change', Mothership, 8 July 2020, https://mothership.sg/2020/07/steve-chia-general-election/

10. Kevin Y.L. Tan and Terence Lee, Voting in a Time of Change: Singapore's 2020 General Election (Singapore: Ethos Books, 2021).

11. Rei Kurohi, PAP's perceived credibility falls, more swing voters in S'pore: 5 key takeaways from IPS post-GE2020 survey, The Straits Times, 1 October 2020, https://www.straitstimes.com/politics/five-key-takeaways-from-the-ips-post-ge2020-survey

Chapter 5

1. The WP's motion was ultimately amended by the People's Action Party (PAP) government to say that "The WP supports this political maneuver to take full advantage of the NCMP seat, even as its secretary-general criticises NCMPs as just 'duckweed on the water of a pond'."

2. WP chief Low Thia Khiang's 'duckweed' analogy takes root in Parliament debate: 6 things about the humble plant, The Straits Times, 30 January 2016.

3. Singapore Parliamentary Reports, Vol 94, 29 January 2016.

4. Singapore Parliamentary Reports, Vol 67 col 693–697, 23 July 1997.

5. Indranee rejects Leong Mun Wai's calls to give opposition MPs more resources in Parliament, says current rules 'more than enough', TODAYonline, 9 May 2023, https://www.todayonline.com/singapore/indranee-leong-mun-wai-more-resources-opposition-rejects-2166611

6. Frequently Asked Questions, Public Service Division, https://www.psd.gov.sg/faq/

7. Singapore Parliamentary Reports, Vol 94, 1 March 2018.

8. See oral interview in Chapter 7.

9. See oral interview in Chapter 7.

10. 看见议王议后, Lianhe Zaobao, 6 April 2014.

11. How Active Are Your MPs in Parliament? Exploring MPs' Attendance and Speaking Count, Kopi, 23 June 2020, https://thekopi.co/2020/06/23/singapore-parliament-performance/

12. NMP Tan Su Shan resigned from PAP before her nomination, TODAY, 11 February 2012; NMP-designate quits Young PAP, TODAY, 9 July 2009; Improving the system for selecting NMPs, TODAY, 17 June 2014; Almost

famous: Former NMP Calvin Cheng has met 90% of people he has fought online in person, Mothership, 5 August 2018.

13. Tan Cheng Bock podcast: NMP scheme "not the right way to enter Parliament", The Independent Singapore, 25 November 2020, https://theindependent.sg/tan-cheng-bock-podcast-nmp-scheme-not-the-right-way-to-enter-parliament/

14. NCMP scheme 'superior to proportional representation', TODAYonline, 28 January 2016, https://www.todayonline.com/singapore/ncmp-scheme-superior-proportional-representation

15. N. L. Aumeerally (2005), The Ambivalence of Postcolonial Mauritius, International Journal of Cultural Policy, 11(3), 307–23.

16. Amar Roopanand Mahadew, The Best Loser System in Mauritius: An Essential Electoral Tool for Representing Political Minorities, in Jaap de Visser, Nico Steytler, Derek Powell, and Ebenezer Durojaye, eds, Constitution Building in Africa (Baden-Baden: Nomos, 2015).

17. Other recent examples of SMCs being merged into GRCs after a close fight at a general election include Fengshan, Sengkang West and Punggol East in the Electoral Boundaries Review Committee report after the 2015 General Election — these SMCs "disappeared" at the 2020 General Election.

18. See oral interview in Chapter 7.

19. It's like 'night and day': Workers' Party MP Gerald Giam on being an MP versus an NCMP, Channel NewsAsia, 14 March 2021, https://www.channelnewsasia.com/singapore/workers-party-mp-gerald-giam-interview-ncmp-aljunied-grc-329101

Chapter 6

1. Frequently Asked Questions, Public Service Division, https://www.psd.gov.sg/faq/

2. Lee Li Lian of the Workers' Party (WP) did decline the offer of an NCMP seat put to her after the 2015 General Election, although that NCMP seat was ultimately "transferred" to Daniel Goh of the WP East Coast Group Representation Constituency (GRC) team, through a parliamentary motion filed by the WP. This incident is covered in Chapter 2 of this book. — Editors

Chapter 8

1. 4 July 2020, https://www.facebook.com/182873625088645/posts/4297580983617868
2. PAP cannot assume that it will form the next government: Lawrence Wong, CNA, 6 November 2022. https://www.channelnewsasia.com/singapore/lawrence-wong-pap-conference-cannot-assume-will-form-next-government-3047901
3. Jeyaretnam says "yes" to offer of NCMP, The Straits Times, 11 January 1997.

Chapter 9

1. Although Barisan Sosialis leader Lee Siew Choh's bizarre call for the opposition to boycott Parliament in 1966 in protest of Singapore's independence certainly did not help.
2. As in Braddell Heights Single Member Constituency (SMC) after the 1991 General Election and Joo Chiat SMC after the 2011 General Election.
3. Navene Elangovan, 'Double standards' in how People's Association and grassroots groups operate in opposition wards: Pritam Singh, TODAYonline, 16 October 2019. https://www.todayonline.com/singapore/double-standards-how-peoples-association-and-grassroots-groups-operate-opposition-wards
4. Amanda Lee, WP charged with using NCMP scheme to showcase its members, TODAYonline, 30 January 2016. https://www.todayonline.com/singapore/wp-charged-using-ncmp-scheme-showcase-its-members

Index